Margaret is a licensed practical nurse, who has enjoyed writing short, real-life stories. This is her first published full-length story and book. Mother of three grown children, she was born in an RAF hospital in Bridgnorth, Shropshire. As a young girl, she moved and lived with her family in Copenhagen, Denmark, before briefly living in Twickenham, England, and then becoming a landed immigrant to Canada with her arrival in Victoria, British Columbia, at the age of four. She now resides in Calgary, Alberta.

For my siblings.

Margaret Godsman

4GIVENESS

M Godsman

Dear Kelsey,
  Our night gardener
who shares how to
create in the secret
of the night.
      Love Rose.

AUSTIN MACAULEY PUBLISHERS™
LONDON • CAMBRIDGE • NEW YORK • SHARJAH

A CIP catalogue record for this title is available from the British Library.

ISBN 9781528930260 (Paperback)
ISBN 9781528966214 (ePub e-book)

www.austinmacauley.com

First Published (2020)
Austin Macauley Publishers Ltd
25 Canada Square
Canary Wharf
London
E14 5LQ

I would like to acknowledge Taylor for her enduring patience with this project. Taylor's editing brought both light and perspective to my deepest memories.

Rose, for her support from the very early days of this story's unfolding. Deb, for her on-going support to have this book published. As well as many individuals who decided to support or oppose this story being told.

Author photograph by Nimmi Godsman.

Cover idea by Jessie Godsman.

'A life that is worth writing at all is worth writing minutely and truthfully.'

– Henry Wadsworth Longfellow

Chapter 1

Victoria, B.C. Oak Bay
Spring 1963

I was hurrying across the Oak Bay High School grounds. The surface at first glance looked both lush and green. Sports played out daily within the lines marked. The field I had come to name 'Sea of Divots'. I had found it was impossible for me to both lengthen my strides and look up at the blue cloudless sky.

Now, as I listened to the first bell, lunch break was over. Any potential last moments for daydreaming in the sun abruptly came to a halt. Not able to run. I took a deep breath and determined a steadfast path toward my school, Oak Bay Junior High.

Thank goodness it was Friday afternoon. It would be more enjoyable for me once the May long weekend began. We celebrated Great Britain's Queen Victoria's birthday, May 24th.

Queen Victoria had reigned over Great Britain as the longest female monarch in history. I felt I had reason to celebrate. I had been born in England and I still felt proud of my ties to my English heritage.

The May holiday Monday came about in Canada long before confederation. In 1845, the first legislation in Canada regarding this event was passed by the Canadian parliament. We saw it as the first weekend to celebrate the beginnings of summer.

The school's end of the day announcements brought closure to my classes. I unfolded myself out of my desk. I am tall for my age, and like many of us, I have to squeeze into those tiny desks provided in grade seven. My agitation retreated as I walked the length of the unlit hallway, swiftly, I stroked the bar that opened the door outside and onto the tarmac. My eyes watered immediately from the bright sun. I turned away from the brightness only to feel the immediate scorching heat burning into the back of my cardigan. I am taking the longer route home in spite of the heat. I want to head to the corner store to buy a popsicle. I normally had to be home right after school, but this particular Friday, I didn't have to rush. I heard my audible sigh as I reminded myself. Cleaning out my desk for the weekend, I had found a dime. My usual intended driving force to get me home subsided.

As I walked away from the school entrance, I saw parked on the main road a distinctly shaped car. I could see the driver stationed in his vehicle. My older brother was into cars. I was reminded of a conversation where my brother was telling Dad what he thought was the difference between American and foreign-built cars. From my memory of their conversation, it was more likely this car was foreign. Moments later, the driver stepped out of his oddly shaped green car. When he turned and faced me, he was smiling. He was headed toward my path. Although we would cross paths, my thoughts had returned to the variety of flavored popsicles. Unexpectedly, I heard what I thought had been the driver calling out, "Hi!" As I turned my head to answer his remark, I instinctively placed a hand on my left eye to block the sun. Not quick enough, I still had to squint. I felt my eye watering and at the same time, I thought to myself that he must want instructions on how to get into the school. I chose to speak to him.

I replied nonchalantly, "Hello." At the same time as I stopped walking, I glanced down at the pavement. I am shy. He quickened his pace toward me. He introduced himself as Dennis Bolton. I barely caught his first name as his appearance suggested he was even older than my brother. Why would I need to know his name? He asked me, "Are you just getting out of school?"

I replied, "Yes, I am."

Somehow this question from him was so obvious to me that it made me smile. He said, "I am here to pick up my brother Rick." He then asked me, "Do you know him? He plays in the school band."

"No," I replied, trying not to laugh. I had no idea who his brother was. I felt myself noticing that Dennis, on the other hand, was cute. Barbara, my girlfriend, was always going out with 'cute guys'.

Dennis asked me, "Do you have any plans for the long weekend?" Now, with much unexpected surprise to his question, I was stumped as to how to reply. I stumbled around to answer, and immediately felt embarrassed. I looked down at my shoes silently, because who cared if you were always expected to be available to babysit your siblings. Had I even stopped tearing up in my left eye? He hadn't seemingly been waiting for my answer. He went on to ask me, "Could you come out to a party Saturday night?"

Still feeling my discomfort over my watering eye, I wasn't answering and Dennis continued to talk. Now he was describing how he had seen me crossing over the high school grounds earlier in the day. "Nobody at the high school," he remarked, "seems to know you by my description." He started to laugh at himself. I thought, *I guess not, since I don't attend high school.*

I didn't find the words to mention this and believed he was in high school. *How old could he be?* I didn't speak. But took the moment to take in what I was being asked.

My mom at that time had been pushing me to date. I still had my dolls stored in a small closet that was part of my upstairs bedroom. I would pass the time sitting on a small trunk inside the closet and remember a time when I had played with them. My mom would interrupt by leaning over the small closet entrance. Her statue blocked any natural light coming in. Then placing her hands on her hips, and with her tone of disapproval, Mom would say, "Beth, if you are to be married by the age of fifteen, you can't play with dolls anymore. Now put them aside." I wasn't even thinking of a real date. Dennis asking me out was okay somehow. I found myself answering with a smile and then spoke, "Yes." I told him I probably could go out. I then went on to tell Dennis if he could phone me after 6 p.m. I would have had time to ask my mom.

Just then, Dennis's brother turned up. He was carrying a case that obviously held a band instrument, not looking cute at all. *Wow, how different can two brothers be?* Dennis's brother's hair was all in his face and his glasses were looking smudged, dirty in fact. His shirttail was half in and half out of his trousers. Dennis introduced his brother, Rick. It gave me an opportunity to introduce myself as well and share my telephone number. Rick's face didn't reveal any emotion. He didn't seem to even notice I was there. He appeared to be studying his brother.

Dennis looked smart and fresh, in stark contrast with his brother. I no longer wanted a popsicle. I was now in a hurry to get back home to call Barbara. I had a date for Saturday night.

When I had barely arrived home, I told my mom I had been invited out for Saturday night and she looked pleased. Later that evening after Dennis called, we went upstairs and looked over my clothes in the closet to see what I could wear. My mother always liked taking pride in purchasing my clothes. Mom loved to see me dress up for an occasion. She brought out from my closet a sky-blue light wool dress lined with no sleeves. I didn't remember this particular dress. Seeing it, I instantly disliked the color. Mom sometimes went ahead and bought clothes without input from me. But as she so often had, she won me over by pointing out the style with the straight skirt and dropped waistband. I can see looking at my mom's facial expressions, she is pleased with herself. We agree this would be a good choice.

I told Mom, Dennis could drive and we were going to a party. Driving with a fellow revealed to her he was quite a bit older than myself. "Oh," my mom replied. I watched as she postured herself, at the same time her eyes dropped to the floor, she then turned herself way from me.

When Dennis arrived at our house the following evening wearing a dress shirt, sweater, topped with a corduroy jacket and met my mom, she smiled. I could tell she approved. While my mom greeted Dennis, it gave me a chance to look at his features. He wasn't much taller than myself. His thick almost black hair was naturally groomed. His brown eyes were twinkling and his mouth showed a great smile with the whitest teeth in contrast to his own Victoria's windy climatic face. Since I had the most awkward teeth, I almost always noticed other peoples' teeth. Moments later, we were walking to his car parked in our driveway. Dennis made a distinct effort to come over to my side of the car and open the passenger door for me. I knew Mom would have liked seeing that before seeing us drive away. The inside of Dennis's car was very clean. The seats felt comfortable and smelled like leather. The dashboard had the same pale muted green color as the outside of the car. I learned through my curiosity the car's make was a Fiat. The Fiat, an Italian make, was similar to a German Volkswagen. Dennis made the comparison, so it wouldn't appear so strange that both vehicles had the car's motor located in the back of the car. Dennis's tone emphasized to me his enthusiasm with his car. The car's motor made a continued humming noise, which became louder when Dennis changed the standard set gears. Our conversations were continually disrupted with the noise as we continued our drive through the Uplands gates.

The Uplands was known as an exclusive residential area just outside of Oak Bay, the community where I lived. On arrival, the house quickly represented itself as a giant amongst the neighboring homes. As the house was located on a hill, the sloping property took on an extraordinary view. While Dennis took off his jacket and placed it neatly on the back seat of his car, we could hear the loud sounding tunes from The Beach Boys' hit song, *Surfin' USA*, Buddy Holly's *Peggy Sue*, and Frankie Avalon's *Venus*. As we began our walk to the festivities, we could take in the ascending view fully. There were tennis courts alongside the pool. Kids were seen in different groups over the expansive lawn. As we took strides upward to the back entrance, the music continued to blare out with songs from Ricky Nelson and Paul Anka. We had to come right up to the house exterior for us to greet anyone Dennis knew to speak to. There were larger groups of kids closer to the house entrance. In the pool, heads could be seen bobbing up and down with brief appearances of bright colored bathing suits. Student laughter came from the guesthouse, and even out of the basement of the main house. This party wasn't just any party of kids. It was the after-graduation party for Oak Bay High School. I startled myself by this observation. I wasn't old enough to recognize anyone from this graduating class. I wouldn't be able to speak to anyone without an introduction. I thought back to my earlier phone call with Barbara. Now I realized why her sister, in grade ten at the high school couldn't recognize either Dennis's name or his description. Dennis casually spoke to one person, and then another person. Sometimes, he would introduce me and I would say, "Hi!" or smile. There wasn't a great need for conversation on the grounds. You could swim, dance, or play tennis. Dennis led me inside where, in the basement, a game of table tennis was being played. Once inside, I heard groups enjoying gregarious outbursts to rally those playing in teams a game of darts. Dennis took the opportunity to offer to get me a drink. I saw many wooden cartons stocking a variety of pop flavors. I loved to drink Orange Crush. Dennis had a Coke. I was really happy to have an Orange Crush to myself. It was a rare treat in my house.

We stayed and watched in part the table tennis game, and the dart game going on nearby. A while later, we wandered back outside to see a pool volleyball game and tennis being played. The sun was still warm for the evenings' activities. There was a rumor that the party had been going on now for almost 24 hours without any noticeable supervision. A predictable answer to why the neighbors were giving hints of getting tired of the loud music. I could see on the horizon vividly, colorfully attired couples in Bermuda shorts, matching shirts with matching colored socks pacing and spanning their properties. At 10 p.m., it was still daylight when the police arrived in their black and white cars. Two cars pulled up alongside the opposite curb and parked. Then, four officers got out of their vehicles. As they approached, crossing the street their distinct walk represented to me officers, appearing to have an easy manner.

The students began to group together where the police had strolled onto the lawn to inquire who was in fact hosting the party. It turned out the student whose house it was, wasn't even home. Someone remarked on the question by telling the officer, "He was already away touring in Europe."

The gathered friends of this student appeared to be listening to the officers' questions. Almost immediately, given the expanding group attendance coming toward the officers, one of the officers began to state in an official tone a noise complaint had been made and advised us to finish up our partying. The students' initiative then became surprisingly boisterous by breaking into the theme song from the Walt Disney's *Mickey Mouse Club* television program, *'M-i-c-k-e-y M-o-u-s-e.'*

As I looked around, I was astonished with this particular song being sung in response to the officer's suggestion of closing down the party. There were now at least fifty teenagers now bolstered on by this initiative outburst of song. Now in addition, the students swayed back and forth in song harmony, continuing loud and clear. The police could no longer be heard and they turned and went back to their black and white vehicles. I watched as the students circled around and followed them to the edge of the property, while retaining their high pitch melody until they drove away. One fellow had yelled out further and called them pigs. I had never heard police called pigs before. I remembered being surprised at this expression for an officer. Everyone was in great spirits after that. It was definitely a feeling of lightheartedness I was experiencing. On the way back to the main house, we were invited to join teams to play lawn croquet. When Dennis dropped me off at home before midnight, he made sure I got into my house. He himself waited at the bottom of the front stairs.

How polite, I thought.

Chapter 2

Summer arrived. I had wanted to pick strawberries in the local farming community like the year before, to earn money to spend. Our neighbors' teenagers were going again and had invited me along. I would have had companionship for the month of July. But my mom had me babysitting my brother Thomas, age five, and my sister Amy, aged two, all summer. My mom worked during the day. I specifically was not allowed to discipline my siblings nor take them out to the beach or park. I had to remain in our house or in the backyard. We made a great number of birds' nests, from the dirt under different fruit trees. We built forts, made picnic lunches, and games were played. Making birds' nests was by far my favorite. Sometimes, I would get involved into the activities so much that I would complete the nest or fort often without my siblings. If I did have additional time alone outside, my mom, just coming out to hang the washing, would disrupt my thoughts. My imagination of a faraway land interrupted. Although nothing verbal was said, I would feel like I was being hovered over. The feeling was so strong and uncomfortable, I would volunteer to return inside to help either with chores or prepare a daily meal. It was my common belief there was never any time to have imagination at home except when I played with my siblings. On the weekend, I cleaned the house with my older brother when he lived here at home but now by myself. Often, Mom sent out the dry-cleaning with the bed sheets to be laundered. Mom smoked cigarettes, drank coffee, and did the washing and ironing on the weekends. In the evening, I was granted time after dinner to visit a friend, go for a bike ride or go for a walk. I did these activities most often by myself, as I only had Barbara as my friend in the neighborhood. My dad was seldom at home. My oldest brother was away in Ontario for the summer with a friend working construction. My brother had a dream of becoming an airplane pilot. He was earning money to get private flying lessons. My oldest sister, Kate, had recently completed her stewardess training in Montreal, Quebec, with Air Canada. Now she was stationed on the mainland in Vancouver, British Columbia, working as an airline stewardess.

On the Wednesday evening prior to the last weekend in August, known as Labor Day weekend, I was granted a holiday to visit my sister Kate in Vancouver. The Labor Day National Holiday Monday was officially granted in 1894. The Prime Minister of Canada at the time, Sir John Thompson, had received ongoing pressure from the working class. In the beginning, the holiday had been used to have meetings on how to improve working conditions. I remember my folks both shared remarks in appreciation for this yearly holiday.

My visit with my sister was considered a treat for all the babysitting I had done during the summer for my mom. My mother relied heavily on me with babysitting because both my older siblings were away. This upcoming event didn't seem much of a treat to me. I wasn't being offered any allowance to spend, and I had to keep a family secret from both my sister and brother.

On my arrival at my sister's apartment, I soon felt relaxed. Her apartment's location was in the west end of Vancouver, overlooking Stanley Park. The view from the 20th floor was remarkable. The extensive view of Stanley Park showed the flowering gardens lining the walking paths. Directly in front while standing on her balcony, I could view the sailboats moored at Vancouver's Rowing club resonating in rows. Colorful tarps covering main sails were reflecting stately figures to me. Alongside the left of the balcony, I viewed steep foliage and natural breadth fir trees. Through the swinging foliage breezes, I could just catch a glimpse and see the Lions' cast concrete heads statues lining the beginnings to crossing onto the Lions Gate Bridge. To the right, less visible as a landmark, was the low-rise Bayshore Inn.

Kate interrupted my viewing from her balcony. She invited me back inside as she couldn't wait any longer to show me her wings pin with the Air Canada logo, she received for completing her stewardess training. She was to wear the pin on her uniform lapel. She was proud of her accomplishment. She made it clear that the stressful part of her training was learning first aid for emergency landings. I was happy for her. In celebration, she took me to the largest Safeway grocery store on Robson Street and had me pick out dessert. I chose a black forest cake. The cake had real whip cream, cherries on top with thin slabs of chocolate. It looked amazing. Back at her apartment, she offered me a sickly B.C. wine to drink. It was fizzy and was named Baby Duck. In her relaxed environment, I mistakenly revealed my mother's secret. My sister had me tell her what was going on while I was drinking. My mother's secret was she would take the opportunity when our dad was sailing on the upcoming long weekend, to move all of us kids with her across town and leave our father. My mom hadn't even revealed to me yet, where in fact, we would be moving to exactly. When my sister asked why I answered apologetically, "I didn't know Mom's specific reason."

I couldn't form into words her specific reason. I knew my folks were for the most part unhappily married. But what exactly was driving my mother's forced action now was unclear to me. Unfortunately, the drinking along with the rich tasting dessert made me vomit in the toilet. It wasn't until morning I realized when I was brushing my teeth, I had thrown up my metal plate with two teeth attached to it. Now I was going to be further in trouble. I would have to begin the new school year with gaping gaps in my front teeth. How was I going to remember instinctively not to smile? A new metal plate with teeth attached would take at least a week after the new molding had been taken. It was too embarrassing for me to register the full impact of the time I may have without my appliance. Not trusting my mom would help with this situation was a further concern for me. I began remembering as well in my altered state I had been unprepared for my sister's questions. It had been my responsibility to carry Mom's secret plan.

I now realized I had been disloyal to Mom. Kate, a half-sister not born to my mom, would of course be loyal to our dad. I hadn't thought about this, I am twelve years old. Dad was scheduled to sailboat race on the long holiday weekend. Dad's pre-occupation with his boat races could possibly occupy his time during Mom's plan to move. I wanted to desperately believe his time would be occupied. To have to see my mother become violent, either to myself or toward my dad, was too awful to imagine. Earlier in the summer, he had told me the final sailboat race standings from this Labor Day weekend, were important to crew members. An award prize ceremony marked the end to the sailboat race season. Although I had whined and cried the night before to my sister about how I didn't want to change schools. How I didn't want to move away from our neighborhood. Now I wanted it to go back to me not having said anything. I was ashamed I had opened up to my sister. When had I ever had any say in my life direction including going to a particular school?

Kate is now on the phone with Dad. I can hear her very distinct English accent detailing the moving arrangement Mom was planning. I now feel I had been set up by my sister to talk details of the move. Dad must have been suspicious of something Mom was planning. Kate was describing her interpretation of the situation. While I listened, I clung to the idea how things could return to before I had exposed my mom's plan. Kate's tone, along with her words and laughter, contained no relevance to the impact this would have on my relationship with my mom. I was now anxiously waiting for Richard to return home. I now felt pressured I would have to go with Mom, having spilled her secret plan.

Richard arrived on a flight from Toronto on Friday during the day. The plan was I would return with Richard on the ferry that evening. We picked him up from the airport and very soon after, found ourselves telling him our mom's plan. Richard flatly refused to accept the move and believed he could convince Mom to stay. He deferred a laugh over my missing teeth.

Chapter 3

Richard described the hardships he endured during the summer over an early dinner for us, and a late meal for him. He was yawning while talking because of both the early to rise to drive from Kitchener to make his flight out of Toronto along with the time change of three hours. Both Richard and his friend, Hans, had lived with relatives of Hans's in a moderate-sized trailer in Kitchener. The trailer was cramped with so many family members having to live in it. The humidity in the town of Kitchener, Ontario during the summer was something Richard had never experienced living on the west coast. He described it as intolerable. Richard and Hans, often left alone to cook their own meals, ate most of their meals out of cans as they were too tired to prepare meals. Laundry was rarely done. He didn't think at times he would survive. He said, "I am not going home to move!" I decided Richard was the one to convince our mom not to go.

That evening, leaving the mainland on the ferry to Victoria, I felt Richard's tension and my relief. I was happy I could share with Richard this burden I had held onto all summer. I leaned over the railing and waved to Kate on the pier. Kate had tried to convey that all would be okay now that our dad was aware. Wishfully, I wanted to believe Richard knowing Mom's plan before going home was helpful for him to convince our mom to stay.

When we arrived at our house, Richard and Mom went and spoke together in the kitchen. I decided to take a backseat and left the room. I retreated into the hallway. I made it to the door leading upstairs to my room then, I heard Mom's tone.

Their heated conversation wasn't going well. I decided I might be trapped going upstairs to my room. I headed quickly further down the hallway toward the front door. This was my usual plan to escape the wrath of Mom's temper. Taking in the seriousness of my plight, I fidgeted with the front door's knob handle. I was too late, as Mom appeared abruptly through an adjacent door into the hallway. She came through the living room, rather than from behind the direction I had anticipated. I wasn't able to make it out the front door. Instead, Mom pushed me away from the door handle and placed her back up against the front door. I ducked as she reached out to grab a hold of me. I had enough time to run into her bedroom. I rushed to the opposite side of her room. I was up against her bedroom window. She was leaning across the bed with her hand stretched out, threatening me with the carving knife. I don't remember what I said. Mom was blaming me for Richard not wanting to come with her. I tried re-tracing my steps swiftly past her. Mom had reached over much further across the bed, I thought. I felt I could race past her before she could recover her balance. I was not quick enough to get past the bottom of her bed and at the same time open the bedroom door, and she soon had me cornered up against her bureau. I heard Mom's high pitch ridiculing voice, and in the same moment I saw the knife coming down on me, inches away from my head. In that second of time, I am feeling total defeat. I instantly knew I had never experienced or felt defeat before. The feeling of defeat was so strong I wasn't able to somehow defend myself. Instinctively, I shrank into the bureau. I could hear the sound of the metal-framed pictures displayed on the bureau toppling over. I had stretched back, further leaning backwards over the bureau until I had myself up against the wall. I looked over at the bedroom door and began to see Richard's fingers curling around and pushing back the door. Richard's decision to come must have been prompted after hearing Mom's rude and coarse language. I hadn't been able to utter any sound to help myself, I felt physically sick. I could see Richard's head as it now appeared around the door. He quickly saw the knife. I watched as he sped to grab a pillow from Mom's bed, while simultaneously reaching out to get a hold of her forearm was all in my sight.

He used brute strength to force a pillow between the knife and myself. Mom must have been surprised and given way for an instant. Then I heard Richard shouting, "Beth, run!" I soon was out the door and headed up the hallway to the stairway heading for my bedroom. I didn't have a lock on my bedroom door but I sat down and had my back up against the door. I listened as hard as I could. I heard someone downstairs go into the bathroom and slam the door. What was going to happen next? I slid up the wall long enough to turn on the switch for the ceiling light in my bedroom. Without curtains, on the windows the bright overhead ceiling light reflected black shadows from the windows onto the walls. I still didn't feel safe, even though this was how my room looked at night and how I often felt. I was reminded of how and when I had made the decision to help my brother by moving into this unwelcoming room. I had in fact given up on ever being a young girl. Dad had deliberately ignored my tenth birthday. He had watched T.V. while I opened my gift from Mom. I had waited until he came home from work before taking the time to open my gift. It had been solid teal blue pants and the shirt had white and teal stripes. He hadn't been interested and continued to watch a T.V. show and eat his dinner. He made the statement during the commercial that he didn't believe in gifts for birthdays. All the while, never even moving his head to glance at me. We were all made to adhere to my dad's harsh own upbringing where his dad hadn't recognized birthdays. Why not say happy birthday? I now had the same sick feeling that had overcome me in that moment. With Dad, I had instinctively felt the barrier between us expand like a pink sponge, slowly filling up with water. The next day, my mom told me she couldn't afford the outfit and she would be returning it to the store for credit. I was in shock by my mom's anger toward me. It was her decision to have purchased the outfit. I seized the moment with my own anger to switch my loyalty to my brother and tell her I wanted to move upstairs to the bedroom across from my brother. Now sitting here listening, I was more interested in what Richard would do next while asking myself at the same time how would Mom harming me help her in her move?

Richard came up quite a while later after the incident. Hearing him, I got myself into bed. Then I heard Mom come upstairs and yell at Richard in his bedroom. I overheard her tell him she was going to take all his belongings with her in the morning. I believe what I heard then was a thump from my brother striking our mom. She had fallen to the floor by the sound of the thump. Mom then left and returned to the main floor, leaving an uncomfortable silence. A little while later, Richard approached me. He knocked gently on my door and entered quietly. Using a whispering voice, he told me, "Beth, it wouldn't be a good idea if you went with Mom." I told him, "I agree!" Although Richard was often a bully in how he usually handled most situations between us, I was thankful for the idea of not having to go. Richard is fourteen years old.

Chapter 4

The next day was Saturday, moving day. Thomas and Amy must have been taken to our grandmother's the day before, to have her babysit during the move. The early morning voice I was hearing was my mom on the phone. Next, I heard her speaking to both Richard and the movers.

My brother, up so early? Was this real? I was now sitting three steps up the staircase, listening to Richard directing the movers. Here was my brother, supervising our mom's arrangements. As usual, either Richard or myself had to be the orchestrators in these situations to produce the results Mom had in mind. Dad, having been equally equipped, was incapable of doing these kinds of tasks. Sitting here on the steps, I was reminded when I was barely six years old and we had moved into this house. Richard and I spent hours wrapping the kitchen plates and glasses in newspaper preparing for our move. Dad had been a willing participant for the move. Watching my brother now, I couldn't remember how Dad had contributed in helping us move our possessions into this house. Mom's weakness was trying to complete and organize tasks in a timely manner. I remembered how, in our last move, she had her brother's help. But I don't think my mom was talking to her brother during this move. So, she wouldn't be able to ask him to help. Mom was always falling out with one of her two siblings. Besides, my mom had more trust in our loyalty for helping with her plans. Unfortunately, Richard or myself were never truly thanked for our participation. Mom's willful competitive nature just wouldn't allow it. I positioned myself to see more, looking through the crack in the hallway door. I wanted to know where Mom was. Not seeing her, I poked my head around the doorway. My brother caught sight of me and called out, "Beth, I think it would be best if we sent everything with Mom." We instinctively agreed we didn't want Thomas and Amy to be without the T.V., couch, kitchen table, and chairs. I feared using my voice. I swallowed hard what felt like spit, and chose nodding as my answer to reply.

Just then, I could see Dad as the front door opened. He had turned up. Richard, then hearing the door opening, turned and began shouting at him angrily, "Dad, just get out of here right now! You aren't going to be having any say of what stays." I waited, scared of what my dad's reply might be. I didn't hear a reply. I think hearing Richard's tone, Dad was relieved to go. I saw my dad on the front door landing, turn himself away from the doorway. He then hesitated before moving to the steps to leave. I am not sure when my brother had expressed to him, we weren't going with Mom. Maybe our sister had told him.

Now in the main hallway, I could hear and had a quick glance to actually see my mom packing up the remains in the kitchen. I now went deliberately to the front of the house. Richard made the decision that both our beds and his dresser would stay. I think it was just after lunchtime when both the movers and Mom left.

Mom hadn't spoken a word to me before she left. Richard and I went into our usual Saturday pattern, he vacuumed and I tidied up. I washed the kitchen counter down and cleaned the bathroom. The vacuum, Ajax cleaner, rags along with the ironing board/iron had been left behind.

Richard came back into the kitchen, taking notice that the cupboards were bare. For some reason, Mom had left the toaster. He yelled out to me, "Beth come here." While holding one of the upper cupboard doors open, Richard turned his face toward me grinning, "How were we going to cook anything?" We then looked into the stove's drawer below the oven and saw it was empty as well. I didn't hesitate with my answer, "I could borrow a pot from our neighbor." Our neighbor who lived behind us, and whom I had babysat for recently.

Now walking down, the basement stairs and heading to the back of our properties where our adjoining gate was situated, I realized it was a gutsy thing to be asking. I was nervous when our neighbor came to their door. First, I smiled at her and then asked, "Hello Mrs. Granger, would it be alright if my brother and I borrowed a pot from you to boil water in?" Mrs. Granger's large blue-gray colored eyes, her best facial feature gave me a puzzled look. She then agreed tentatively. Her very red lipstick lips began to give a turned down frown. Her response quickly warned me that I wasn't feeling calm. I had to hide how shy, in fact, I was in asking for this favor. When she returned, I knew by her steadiness she had been told something. I hid my fear by taking a deep breath and forcing a smile again. Mrs. Granger replied to my smile with a question. "So, has your mom moved?" Her tone high in pitch was blunt. I focused on watching her red lips curl over her protruding front teeth, and volunteered that I was staying with both my dad and my brother. Before I turned to leave, I thanked her for the pot and her help. She called out, with a disapproving tone as I turned and walked back into our yard. "Beth, you can't babysit for us any longer." I didn't turn and look back. Soon after I heard much clanging of pots before I was back home behind closed doors.

Richard and I boiled water in the pot and ate a boiled egg with toast, and Richard drank the remaining milk from the bottle. Richard said, "I can go to the grocery store near our school." I nodded, and agreed to go with him. He was sitting on the floor, leaning up against the kitchen cupboards staring at the oven. My brother looked tired from the morning's events along with enduring his hardworking summer.

He had savings from his summer earnings so we could buy a few items. He had a purpose for his savings, to take lessons to learn to fly. His face appeared grim and his voice was resonant with his deep anger for Dad. He made the remark, "I certainly plan on getting reimbursed from Dad."

I took a short nap as I recognized the only books that remained were a set of encyclopedias, we used for school projects and Dad's less popular trash, sex scandal books. Dad had kept titles like *'Lady Chatterley's Lover'*, *'Sons and Lovers'* in his den. He defended the author D.H. Lawrence, but it was Dad's ominous behavior that curtailed me to see the lot as anything more than mere trash in describing women with men. Dad had a cot in his den and I, on more than one occasion, had to go in and recover my sister before she was a year old half-dressed and change her diaper. Once I had found blood in her diaper. I remember saying to her she had to stay away from Dad. I had mentioned this occurrence to Mom. I don't remember my mom making any comment. Mom had even gone so far as to take Dad's cot and sleeping bag in the move. Dad had been sleeping in the den for some time when he was home. Mom had that and all my dolls for Amy and so the small upstairs closet was bare as well.

Now back from Safeway after carrying the groceries in silence together, the day seemed to be over. Richard and I had an unspoken way of being comfortable together in our silence.

We boiled hotdogs in the pot for supper. We looked through Dad's camping utensils for plates and cups in the basement. Dad hadn't unpacked fully from his last time out. Typical of how our dad looked after stuff. It was a rumpled mess of all his gear. The tent, rope, canvas and camping utensils, and cook wear all lumped together. It smelled damp. Still we uncovered usable cutlery, melamine bowls, plates, and cups. The frying pan and pots had dried on moldy food particles. Richard angrily threw those away in the tinned garbage cans at the back of our house. His rage I felt with the clanging of lids onto the metal garbage cans. Now we had two days to fill before school started.

Chapter 5

I slept that first night without much thought of the previous night. The following morning, I got up and went for a walk on the beach. Willows beach in Oak Bay was about four blocks away. I hadn't had a morning walk along the beach with the tide out with mine being the first footprints this whole summer. It felt vacant, as if I was being mirrored having little reflection of interest, even here by the sea. I was relieved I didn't have to do so much work just now but I had no thought of what I could be doing.

When I returned, Richard was up and we had a mix of breakfast and lunch. Richard then left to visit a friend. I had watched him walking away before wondering what I could be up to next. I lay around getting used to the idea of not doing the same tasks I had been doing all summer. Cutting up potatoes, and carrots for dinner and making canned soup and sandwiches for lunches for myself, Thomas and Amy. I didn't have the imagination then to allow myself to look at the situation beyond a temporary misunderstanding. I was still feeling anxious how events had unfolded.

I moved my thoughts to be in anticipation for school. I was looking forward as well to visiting with my girlfriend, who was currently on holidays with her family.

When my brother was at home, we spent most of the weekend quietly watching for any reaction from the neighbors. Mrs. Granger's husband was a Royal Canadian Mounted Police officer. R.C.M.P. officers were known as a regulating force to ensure security for the Federal and National policing of Canada. The question remained, could he as an official person have influence on what Richard and I were doing? We were basically living alone, unsupervised by an adult. How long would it take Mom to tell our neighbor that Dad wasn't living here either? Richard took the initiative to cut the front lawn. It had been a hot summer so there was no need to rake. I watched him while standing in the front living room window. I had no interest in weeding the empty flowerbeds. I had spent too much of the summer doing that already.

Chapter 6

I woke up to the sun bright in my room. I stumbled kicking off the covers trying to get up so quickly, I almost slipped on the hardwood floor. I held myself up by reaching out, grabbing a hold onto the doorframe. Then, I almost fell when I tried to skip stairs as I frantically ran down to the main floor. Richard had the same habit as Mom of keeping all the doors into the hallway and downstairs bedrooms closed. This made the hallway dark. I was barely awake, yet I knew I was being angrily loud and noisy as I opened the door into the kitchen. The only clock in the house was on the kitchen stove. My heart was beating so fast and with the bright sunshine reflecting off the stovetop metal surrounding the clock, it was making it difficult to read the time. I sighed with relief. I couldn't believe my good luck. The time was ten minutes past seven o'clock. My friend Barbara wouldn't be coming down the street for another hour. I took a deep breath. I had plenty of time to get ready for school. I started in the bathroom so as not to get into my brother's way when he got up. I had my toothbrush in the medicine cabinet along with Richard's. I noticed an old rusty looking razor with a blade. I reflected on whose razor had it been. Had it been my mom's or possibly my dad's. It was the only remaining personal daily reminder of our folks. When had Dad removed all his clothes and belongings? Had that gone unnoticed by me with all the moving? No tooth-powder. I sighed deeply, I remembered Mom used to brush her teeth with salt and water sometimes.

I now searched all the kitchen cupboards and found a half-opened box of salt.

Absent-mindedly, I poured a small amount into my left hand and went back and dipped my toothbrush in the salt and brushed my teeth. It had an awful taste. I rinsed my mouth several times by cupping my right hand. This wasn't going to be easy to do every day. I forced myself to move to the linen cupboard, and by reaching far into the back of the shelf I found a bar of Ivory soap and an extra towel to hand dry my hair. After I finished having a bath and washing my hair, I had steamed up the window. Opening the frost tint window and looking out into the backyard, I felt stillness everywhere. I saw no movement from the house behind. I don't know why I felt uneasy. I distracted myself by making sure my dress was pressed. After getting dressed I ate my Rice Krispies' cereal standing up leaning against the kitchen sink counter. I spent my time, while I swallowed, watching the clock on the kitchen stove. I still had time to go upstairs and watch from my bedroom window for Barbara and her sister. Barbara's sister, Rachael, met up with her girlfriend one door from mine. They were in high school.

As I opened my bedroom window a crack to listen for my friend, I was feeling anxious having to stand awkwardly looking out from my upstairs bedroom window. I lost track of time briefly. I was anxiously remembering if I hadn't woken in time, how I would have had to explain our circumstances to Barbara before I was ready to accept them myself. I was brought back to the present hearing Richard getting up. Almost immediately, I heard girls' voices as they turned the corner from Bowker Ave. to St Ann Street. I could hear Rachael's voice as she spoke loudly to nearby neighbors. Marjorie and Susan were on the opposite side of the same street coming toward me. I could actually see Marjorie and Susan. As soon as I spotted Barbara, I ran downstairs yelling goodbye to my brother. I went out the door carrying my new scribbler and pencil case.

I knew Barbara would be full of talk about her family trip to the interior of B.C. in the Okanogan. Her new fall clothes and what her boyfriend was up to. I listened to her cheerfulness and looked at her happy face. Her eyes sparkled with laughter. It was delightful for me. She made it easy for me to not have to reply in words. Barbara said to me, "We had such a lovely time with our dad and his speed boat. We could go so fast." Barbara further remarked on how she had even learned how to water-ski. She explained how the weather was so warm you didn't need to worry about falling into the water at Christina Lake. *Wow*, I thought, *that would have been a good way to pass the last of the holidays.*

Christina Lake was originally known as a fishing ground for the tribes surrounding the Okanagan. One of the few tribes Sinixt, Sanpoil traded with the fur trader Angus McDonald. Angus McDonald ran the Hudson's Bay Company's trading post, in the mid-1800s. Christina was the name of the fur trader, Angus's daughter.

Listening to Barbara's stories gave me hope that I could soon be lost in the daily life of school again. We were allowed two electives. Mine were art and music combined, and home economics. Barbara would be taking typing/shorthand and bookkeeping. Barbara wants to be a secretary when she graduates. I don't want to decide anything about my future. We are just going into grade eight. My mom had told me I could become either a dietician or a nurse. Those options seemed very unimaginative to me.

Barbara and I weren't in classes together. In my opinion, I didn't have any other friends that I could count on. Still, back in homeroom class, everyone still liked me somehow. My name had been offered up for the second year in a row to be student president representative for my class. Even if I was to be the student president representative again, I didn't know what I could do to help anyone.

Through the same system as last year, I watched as my name was put forth and written up on the chalkboard. I thought for sure everyone would have seen me as different and not vote as they had last year. The homeroom teacher had us put our heads down on our desks. We then put up our hands when we heard names we wanted to vote into as student council members. The desks smelled like old stale varnish. I remember my stomach felt tight. When we raised our heads, students were turning their heads in my direction. I was voted in once again as class president. I smiled, remembering to keep my mouth closed. Maybe this year I could offer more than just reporting what had been conducted at the monthly meeting. But seriously, the ninth graders had all the say.

Chapter 7

Barbara and I rarely walk home from school together. Barbara has a boyfriend, and he usually walks Barbara home. My usual routine had been to rush home anyway. My brother and sister were being babysat. I had to relieve the babysitter and take over and start dinner. The babysitter was usually grumpy, she was a mother herself and probably wanted to be home for her children when they arrived after school. Still, I would find her in the kitchen sitting at the kitchen table reading her book. The door to the dining room would be closed. Amy was napping in the living room in her playpen. Thomas was in his room also napping. It wasn't like my siblings were giving her trouble. If I had come home even five minutes later than expected, she would speak to me rudely. If I was on time, she was silent. Right after she left, my mom would call and give me instructions for dinner. My mom never asked anything about my day. She just gave the instructions and hung up.

I didn't want to speak to anyone on the way home from school. I could barely make my new way of life make any sense. I looked around me as I walked home. I didn't see anybody. I couldn't bear anyone to know how I was living alone with my brother. I stared down at the pavement, and noticed the cracks and the unevenness of the walk. My mind was still so full of duty, loyalty, and my directed tasks of what I had been to my family. I felt I could hardly breathe. It felt strange how everything was around me but walking home remained the same. I didn't have enough to do at home that would fill all my time. Nothing I did now at home felt familiar to me.

I now had time for homework. Before, I didn't have any time until dinner was over. Between returning from school and eating dinner, preparing vegetables, and playing with my siblings took all of my time. When Dad arrived home, he went into the television room, delaying dinner while he watched the evening news cast on CBS with Walter Cronkite. Dad angrily refused to come to the dinner table until the news program was over. In the meantime, I helped with Amy's dinner. I would feed her while she was in her high chair. After dinner sometimes, I was asked to help with bathing my siblings. Then Richard and I had to do the dishes. Mom helped by putting the leftover food away. Richard being competitive, liked to have me play Ping-Pong with him. He would want to play for the 'winner' not having to do any dishes. I would lose. Then I had all the dishes to do. I really didn't feel like doing homework afterwards. Often when Richard was in a good mood and school was easier for him, or he had scored during one of his soccer matches, he would make the time to have a lengthier game between us.

Richard hadn't helped with babysitting in the afternoons. When he came home, he just shut himself off in his bedroom. Presumably, Richard was studying and doing his homework.

I would sometimes have free time on Sunday, if Amy, now two years old, napped. Mom hadn't been working evening shifts at the hospital anymore. My mom had a job in a doctor/surgeon's office as office manager and bookkeeper.

Now, today I was living with one pot without a lid, a toaster, two knives, forks, spoons, and plates from Dad's leftover camping utensils. I could make a sandwich or boil an egg.

Richard surprised me and came home faster than I expected. He had gone to the Safeway by the school before coming home and bought us more food. He bought frozen vegetables, steakettes, as well. Steakettes were frozen patties of ground beef. I hadn't eaten them before but Richard had learned about them while he had worked the summer months in Ontario. We needed a frying pan to cook those. Richard had found one at Safeway. He had bought ketchup and milk as well. We were feeling pretty good. We now had cereal or toast for breakfast, peanut butter and jam sandwiches for lunch, mixed frozen vegetables, steakettes or hot dogs for dinner. Richard said, "We are still limited by our cooking utensils." Richard went on to say, "Dad is planning on coming on the weekend to help." Richard's voice resonated his encouragement with Dad offering his help. Listening to Richard's voice made me feel lighthearted, almost cheerful.

Unexpectedly, the phone rang. I answered from habit then felt frightened when I discovered it was our neighbor. Mrs. Granger was asking if we went to school today. I told her we both had attended school. Mom must have been asking about us. Then she said, "Beth, you can keep our pot for now." I thought I would start crying, hearing Mrs. Granger's tone, but luckily, I didn't. When I hung up, I sighed in relief. I heard myself telling my brother, "Boy, I sure was happy Mrs. Granger hadn't asked about Dad." I didn't want to think what her R.C.M.P. husband might do if he knew Dad wasn't living with us. Richard didn't reply. Maybe Richard wasn't worried anymore, now that he had figured out how to stay here.

Chapter 8

The week at school had continued with the usual beginnings. Assembly for all the grades had started the week. At lunchtimes, I went home. On Wednesday, I had the first student council meeting at lunch held in a classroom. I had remembered my peanut butter sandwich but without wax paper to wrap it in or a serviette, it was messy. I had, on arrival at school, quickly grabbed toilet paper from the school bathroom. The school's toilet paper came in square panels folded and had a shiny surface. Now having used the paper to have my sandwich sit uncovered in my locker, the bread had dried out near the crusts. I figured out I had loaded the bread with too much peanut butter. I did that because I was always so hungry at lunch. I started having a coughing episode. I ended up having to run to the water fountain in the hallway to recover. Now, I had missed events being reported. I would have to ask someone. I felt uncomfortable returning to the classroom or approaching anyone to ask for help.

The newly voted in student council president looked up and saw me returning and volunteered an explanation. I had mainly missed the introduction of ourselves and what grade we represented. *Straight forward enough.* School pictures would be taken in the coming weeks. It was up to us to make sure the students in our homeroom class were reminded closer to the date. We were to request a class list from our teacher to confirm spelling names correctly. Also, volunteers would be needed to help with spontaneous photos for the yearly annual.

We, the class reps, were to volunteer our time in preparation for a school dance to be held on a Friday afternoon in the fall sometime. Teachers needed a date and time so they could be available for supervision. I was certainly curious for what the music selection was going to be. Many 45 vinyl records were going to be needed for sure.

We looked at a calendar and pretty much set a schedule similar to the previous year. All of our ideas would have to be submitted early enough for both approval and for teachers to volunteer their time.

Chapter 9

With the grade nine representatives in charge, the note-taking was minimal. Still, I would have to prepare something. My homeroom teacher was a stickler for a report. When I began speaking, most of the students listened attentively. But I couldn't understand their stares. This was making me feel uncomfortable. Why did my classmates keep staring at me? I went back after reporting and sat at my desk feeling nervous. Of course, the reason they were staring at me was my missing teeth. I probably had forgotten not to smile. I was waiting for an appointment next week to have my plate with the two teeth on it replaced. I would have to find out how to take the bus and get there by myself. But I had an appointment for the following week. I was very thankful. I was being granted permission to rectify the loss of my appliance. I am not sure but I assumed that through Kate's help, Dad had passed on the information to make the necessary appointment.

I had teeth that when the second set grew in, they appeared similar to a second set of baby teeth. I still had the beginnings of a third set in my gums. To even out my teeth and encourage the third set to come down, the dentist took out my incisor teeth and I wore a plate with those two teeth on them.

When my mom was not beating me with a yardstick but still angry, she would make me take my plate out of my mouth. I had to hand it over to her for an undetermined amount of time. It was extremely humiliating. I would worry she wouldn't give it back for school or a planned activity. She complained bitterly how much this had cost her.

I had to constantly be aware not to smile. If I did smile, it would remind my brother to call me Dracula. It was my brother's favorite nickname for teasing me. He would threaten me with his words, "Talk like that and your teeth are going to fall out." This would embarrass me and I would stumble over my words. This had a lasting effect on me. I rarely smiled, as I would be concerned that my plate with the two teeth might fall out.

Our dentist was my mom's best friend's husband. When I did get to the arranged appointment, would my dentist make any comment about losing my appliance?

Chapter 10

My stickler homeroom teacher, also my English teacher, was so predictable with his first essay assignment for the year. "What did I do over my summer vacation?" How many years had I lied to make up a believable story for my summer vacation? I was sure by grade eight there could be an alternative topic. Nope, same topic that had to be lied about one more time. Now, Friday afternoon, last class English, I was thinking about using Barbara's vacation and her story of events. Barbara had shared how a newly opened golf course near Christina Lake boasted black sand for their sandpits. That might pass as an interesting fact I had learned. Barbara didn't have my English teacher.

So far school had been predictable. I was relieved and happy, knowing the weekend was upon us. I would have to memorize my French verbs. Still, I felt lucky. Most of the schoolwork in the past week had been a review from the previous year's work. My thoughts were interrupted with the final 3 p.m. announcements and then we, the students, would be free. Most of the announcements reflected what forms we needed to be signed. I stared down at the floor, while sitting in my desk with my legs outstretched into the aisle waiting for the announcements to be over. I had to think about how I would forge my mom's signature. How else could I get a signature for these forms? Dad's signature was too difficult to forge. I had to figure out a pen as well. Dad hadn't left his fountain pen. Richard might have bought himself a fountain pen. Really? This was my most anguished problem? Interrupting my thoughts, I was surprised to hear my name was announced to pick up a message at the office. Now what could this message be about? I hadn't any indication this past week any authority had known about my brother and myself living without adults. I wondered why my brother's name hadn't been called instead.

Students or teachers hadn't paid attention while I nervously walked to the main level and office. I had felt the week went fairly well? All things considered. What indeed could this message really change? I didn't believe the school could in fact do anything about the recent changes, or could they?

On entering the school's office, my aunt who was the secretary for the principal, directed me without words to the office's black desk phone. I had completely forgotten Aunty June, my mom's cousin, worked at the school. She had lifted and placed the phone on the counter for me to use. The receiver had been laid down beside the base of the phone, ready for me to pick up. My aunt was standing back from the counter up against the window, presumably out of hearing range.

This kind of message I had not expected. Who in fact would call me at the school? My aunt did not speak to me, or call out my name to direct me to the phone. But instead, pointed with her bright colored nail-polished finger for me to pick up the phone. I said, "Hello." It was Mom. Mom flew into her monologue. She had picked up the rest of the furniture in the house, along with the washer and dryer, and all my clothing. She ended by saying she wanted me to know before going home. I had not said one word, other than hello. Her tone had reminded me of when she would have called after school and given me instructions on what to prepare for dinner. I heard no emotion of concern for me in her voice. I felt no invitation from her either.

I was stunned. When I hung up the phone. I slowly became aware of my aunt sitting now and watching for my reaction. I had the forthwith to thank my aunt, as manners were required. I am not sure why I waited before leaving the office. My aunt gave no facial expression that she knew exactly what my mom had said to me. Moments later, I saw my aunt get up out of her desk chair, she then turned her head a way to look out the window. When she turned further away from me, I noticed she was wearing a floral print blouse that had the same bright color of her nail polish. She went into the principal's office. I left the main office. Walking in the main hallway, I recognized my aunt hadn't reported our situation to our school principal. It had been years since I had been to Aunt June's home. I had, on occasion, slept over and learned how to make homemade cinnamon buns for breakfast. I remembered her as having a gruff side to her as well. Certainly, I was reminded of it today. Though that particular overnight visit I remember her being softer. My mom had explained to me her gruffness was because her husband was difficult at times. Oh yes, and then I remembered how he was a retired R.C.M.P. officer. Finally, it was registering, I was being reminded. My brother and I were on our own.

Chapter 11

I went back to my locker to get my homework. I took deep breaths. On the walk back in the hallway, my brother passed by me, I had heard footsteps coming toward me while focusing on the tiled floor. Lifting my head, I noticed his small smile as he turned his head to look at me briefly in passing. I thought how strange as I noted there weren't any other students in the hallway but us. His back to me now, I thought for a moment I could possibly call out to him, but as I turned fully around to address him, he was already descending on the stairway. My brother had such rigid rules when we were in any public situation, I knew to leave him alone. The necessary walk to my locker included a further flight of steps up to the joining corridor. It took all my gangling strength while using the banister to grip onto, to make it up without tripping over myself. My head was spinning, still too fast for my brain. When I tried opening my locker, the combination lock took many turns. Listening with the lock open, I stood in front of the open locker and steadied myself. Nothing came to mind to take out of my locker. I began to be aware that my homeroom teacher Mr. MacDonald was behind me. I then made a point of standing up straight and looking like I was doing my normal routine. I took the obvious Math, English, Social, and French textbooks. I tried to breathe without sighing. I kept repeating to myself, *What do I need*? When Mr. MacDonald had come to stand behind me and across the hallway initially, I hadn't heard him. Now hearing him clearing his throat, I heard him start back across the hallway until he reached his classroom door. He stopped, and proceeded to watch me peripherally. Mr. MacDonald had this habit of putting the end of his glasses in his mouth and watching you sideways at the same time. He then placed his other hand neatly in his pocket or behind his back. I instinctively knew I had to glance his way and smile, as I shut the locker and I said, "Have a good weekend, sir." He turned and faced me, nodding. As he turned away, I was finally free from being watched.

I walked slowly to the exit sign, taking cautionary steps while descending on the staircase, then the landing and then the second set of stairs. Now, I walked along the hallway to the exit doors that led to the back of the school. Not a single person. I put all my strength into pushing the bar to open the school's doorway. With the opening of the door, the sun was immediately bright and hot. Coming from the darkened hallway, I was blinded and could not see anything or anyone. Added to this, I was too warmly dressed. I cut across the vacant parking lot and gravel pathway. Walking faster now, I stirred up the dust in the gravel. Looking down, I noticed the former shine to my shoes was being replaced by the covering of gravel dust. I steered myself toward the back of the joining property near the high school where I knew the ravine and creek began. Here, the trees were a welcome relief from the sun. My delay in leaving meant I was alone. I found myself trying to manage the weight of my books and my thoughts.

Damn it, Mom had won.

Chapter 12

How and why Mom continued with her behavior, I did not want to know or accept. I had broken out in a sweat. I felt dizzy. My knees gave way and I sat down briefly but there was no relief in doing so. I continued taking the route that went along the ravine, delaying further my need to join the main street. When I came up the side of the steepest part of the ravine and back on the main street, it was empty of any students. Although having taken this longer route, I was hopeful Richard would be home by now, but he wasn't. I slammed the front door on entering and now was striding toward the back of the house into the kitchen. Having arrived into the middle of the kitchen, the sun greeted me brightly coming through the kitchen windows. I turned my head to the window where our neighbor's house vacantly stared back an empty back porch. I wondered to myself, *Had anyone noticed my mom back in the house today*? I decided to make myself a snack. I glanced over the counter tops while reaching to open the overhead kitchen cupboards. I even look in the bottom cupboards. I know full well they are still empty. My mind wouldn't register the emptiness. Absently, I found the cupboard that we keep the tins of peanut butter and jam in. I let out an audible sigh. The sigh brings me back to my decision to make a snack. *Just make a sandwich,* I tell myself. I had eaten so many peanut butter toasted snacks this past week, I couldn't taste anything. Just making the motion to swallow the thickness of the peanut butter was all I could take in. The closed doors on the main level reminded me there was nothing for Mom to take here. So upstairs I went. Entering my room, I see the only thing left behind. The beginnings of a vanity table my Uncle George had made for me. Walking

47

across my room I now drop toast crumbs while looking over the wood top, faint pink painted wood. I was reminded how my mom had me scrub it with Ajax cleaner until the paint was faded and almost gone. She had felt Uncle George's choice of pink paint was too bright a pink. Now, turning and looking back across the empty room I see the dust remains after my bed had been removed. My eyes quickly scanned over the open wall of closet space my uncle had built-into the bedroom. I can find no clothes for school, not even my winter coat, extra sweaters or skirts. I find on a shelf a pair of old pants and a pullover top. Mom had not left anything I might have valued. Not one personal item was left for me. Silver teaspoons I was gifted from her sister, my Aunt Mabel for my collection, or a chain with a small child's locket on it, all gone. Immediately, because of feelings of shame, I fantasized a way to explain to my aunt not having them. I wanted to instantly minimize the situation by saying perhaps they had been offered to my younger sister. As I had these thoughts pouring into my head, I quickly recognized in myself I didn't want to believe for the sake of my aunt, Mom would take my family gifted belongings. I was familiar with my mom's "everything is mine" behavior. Did my aunt know her to behave in this manner as well? I had spent years hiding from the relatives how my mom treated Richard and myself. Mom would have taken the clothing of worth so she could sell them at the secondhand store. Moving to the list of items left; underwear, old clothes, and, right at the back of the hanging closet, an old wearable summer dress.

I changed into the remaining old pants and pullover sweatshirt. I went over and looked in Richard's room. Richard still had his bed and his folded clothes from the bureau had been left on his bed. His bureau gone. Mom had left all his model airplanes on the floor. I was initially frightened as I walked over to his closet. It felt cruel to me what she had done to his prized possessions. I saw he still had his hanging clothes, shirts, and pants. My fear turned to worrying, if now Richard would give up and go live with Mom. My account into these discoveries, illuminated she had failed to mention

48

specifically, taking my bed. So now not having even a bed she continued in my mind, to blame me…

Chapter 13

I waited patiently for the beginnings of evening and the return of Richard. Once the sky began turning to twilight, I decided Richard wasn't coming home anytime soon. I had laid down on the wall-to-wall carpet in the living room waiting, for what exactly? I decided I would go to the beach. On the way, darkness settled in. I decided ending my life would be easier than having to come up with a plan on what to do next. Yes, the week had been what I could best do for myself. Nothing more seemed possible. I didn't even feel I could cry. What would have been the point? Not one person, who I had known as an adult, showed any remorse or concern. Did Aunt June at the school understand my mom's behavior? Did she think these recent events were acceptable? Had my mom given her a specific account of events so that she decided to not interfere? Did it outwardly appear as a temporary fallout between a mother and daughter? I couldn't understand how my mom thought, by taking every personal item of mine, that this would endear her to me. I couldn't comprehend a civil outcome from these further steps she had taken. I couldn't remember any hint of why she would be so determined with her actions at this time. What was her driving force other than her need for a babysitter for our siblings? Even if I returned to live with our mom, would Richard always be available to protect me from her scathing temper? If my mom thought to simply brush over these recent events, would it appear as if I had been stubborn? I felt cornered by my mom's reaction.

I had decided the easiest thing to do was to drown myself. When I got to the beach, the tide was in and it was easy for me to slip off my runners and wade in. For some reason, I decided not to take off my clothing. Ah yes, the thought did cross my mind that any additional weight, would help tire me out so I could drown more easily.

Swimming was always easy for me and I swam, and actually liked how I could swim. I began to feel better. I found myself standing up and rolling up my sleeves while I thought of going back and facing what I would need to do next on my own. I could not reconcile to my thoughts, so I went back to swimming. Was I too stubborn to go back to Mom?

I swam until, when I turned to look back, I could hardly make out the shoreline. I started treading water and waited to become tired. The water was over my head now. I wasn't aware of the temperature of the water. The ocean was never warm. I listened and heard a soft swishing onto my neck and occasionally onto my earlobe. I saw at a distance, a light in someone's living room come on. Still, I wasn't dissuaded from my intention.

I started to feel anger while treading water. Why was it I had to end my life when adults were behaving shamelessly? I reminded myself of the time when we had taken counseling as a family. Mom and Dad would say something in the meeting and then, at home, they both turned their backs on what could have been used to help us as a family. Continuing to tread water, I remembered the time I had confronted my dad on an issue brought up by the counselor. It was something about me having to do all the family dinnertime cooking. The counselor suggested this was another way we did not support one another. The counselor said here was a clear example of how both, my mom and I, needed my dad's support. That evening after the counseling session, I found Dad eating cheese and crackers at the kitchen table. I brought up again what the counselor had said. Dad didn't look up to face me but told me in a cruel, harsh tone to dry up. He then got up from the table and walked into his den. I followed him. I went on to say if he would just not have to watch the news at dinnertime. I spoke gently, saying how eating while the dinner was hot with the family would help. He then turned and faced me, and called me a slut. Huh, as shocked as I was by his tone, I didn't even know then what that word meant. I then turned my back on him and left the room. I knew then in my heart. It was impossible for my folks to see their depth of hate for each other. Despair began to take its grip over me when shortly after, the family counseling meetings ended. I remembered it was as if once the twilight entered on Monday evening and our scheduled family meetings ended, darkness descended heavily upon us. As kids, we were lost at sea. Mom and Dad continued playing a poisonous mind game between them. Neither one admitting what each of them had contributed to the bleakness we endured. Instead, they turned their anger on to us, either ignoring us or making snide remarks. My mom and my dad were not persons I respected or even liked. Why should they be the reason for my failings? Yes, I was isolated and alone. The decision to live was stronger than I would have expected. I didn't feel the same defeat as when my mom had tried to kill me. I felt stronger than I had felt then. And if by some miracle I could survive Mom, she would not have won after all. I don't remember exactly, but I began seeing the shoreline outlining the stony beach more clearly and realized I was swimming back to shore.

I was immediately thankful for getting back to the beach. I waited until the last possible moment before getting to my feet, stumbling to find my footing with my bare feet. The wind felt colder now, I shivered while dripping from my weighted down wet clothing. Picking up my shoes, I listened hard for sounds of someone or something. I heard nothing, not even the sea. I wasn't sure what sounds I might hear at this time of night. I didn't even wait to put on my shoes. I started back to the house. Moving onto the pavement mixed with gravel, I heard a neighboring house shut a door. Startled by this noise, I took in the location of oncoming cars, remaining as much out of sight as I could while I crossed over the main road. Their headlights could bring attention to my state. Two and half blocks away from the beach with my wet clothes, I felt the chilled cold air surrounding me. My hair smelled of saltwater and my hands reeked of seaweed. I started to shake my head and worry about being seen. I picked off kelp that clung to my shirt and the back of my hand. What a sight I must have been. The boulevard's grass gave me an easy way for me to clean off the sand on my feet. I used the city trees to help shield me from any close-up passenger view with the continued oncoming traffic. I turned down a street I didn't live on. I bent over holding onto my shoes and moved furtively along the curb. This particular street I had chosen didn't have sidewalks. It was completely empty of any kind of movement, outside of the wind. Now, I was at the corner of our R.C.M.P. neighbor's front yard. I kept my head down low, while walking under their children's bedroom window. The window blind was open. The children's nightlight was on. The limited light led me first to see my shadow, and then myself following nervously. I walked stiffly from feeling so cold, still bending over on our common path into my backyard. I so wanted to be invisible. The joining property gate latch seemed incredibly loud when shut. My shivering seemed to create noise. I then quickened my pace on our path until I was under our deck. I hadn't been breathing. Taking a deep breath, I listened… still no one home. I entered through the basement door. In the silence I felt comfortable to take off my outer clothes. I placed them on the washing sinks. Yes, the washer and dryer were gone. At the side of the sink, I found my school gym shorts and shirt. I grabbed them. The washer and dryer gone didn't have the same effect as when I first learned about the rest of my belongings being taken. I tiptoed upstairs, arriving at the kitchen. Dripping wet hair onto my shoulders, feeling the coldness. I glanced at the kitchen stove's light. The clock hands' illumination told me it was half past ten. I grabbed a towel on my way up to my room and changed into my sport shorts and shirt. The thought crossed my mind, *Mom must have thought they were Richard's.* I returned to the main floor and instinctively looked at the bottom of the linen closet and found some old blankets we had used for outdoor picnics. I made up a bed for myself on the wall-to-wall carpet in the living room. I waited further for my brother to come home.

Chapter 14

Finally, Richard came home. He had been with his friend, Alan, who could drive. They arrived together. I could hear them in the kitchen together. I couldn't wait any longer. I ran into the kitchen and blurted out what had happened at school. I gave the list of what was missing when I returned home. Richard was beside himself with fury. Richard didn't even check upstairs. He immediately picked up the phone receiver on the kitchen wall. Until that moment, I hadn't noticed Mom had tried pulling out the phone from the wall socket. Richard was even angrier in his attempt to call our dad. Why did I feel responsible for not noticing the phone had been pulled out from the wall? Why did I feel I could have gathered this further information and warned him? Did I feel responsible somehow? My brother was going to have to take on our plight because I could not think of any solution on my own. No answer with his call to Dad. He then called Kate, in Vancouver. He told Kate he was going over right now and getting the furniture back.

Sitting on the kitchen floor with the bright ceiling kitchen light on, I found myself watching Alan's eyes. They were as big as saucers. I watched Alan's expression, and beyond his initial surprise, his posture was stoic. An expression I wasn't familiar with, it was not easy to describe. Alan was somehow showing me that he was familiar with suffering. He couldn't believe how his friend Richard was behaving. Richard had continued shouting angrily into the phone. Now, he abruptly slammed down the phone. He explained to us. Kate, our mom's sister and our uncle, were coming over to the island from Vancouver on the Ferry in the morning. They planned to arrive just before noon. My sister insisted she would come and help get the furnishings back. Richard concluded he had told her he would wait until tomorrow. Then, very unexpectedly, I heard Alan say in a very deep voice with stoic resonance reflecting the gravity of the situation, "Richard, I will come in the morning and drive you." I looked up at my brother and saw from his expression he had been heard by his friend. Richard's anger started to subside. I then asked Richard, "Do you have either Mom's phone number or her address?" He answered looking at the floor, that he didn't have Mom's phone number, but had remembered her address when she had confirmed it with the movers. He then looked across at me to say he felt pretty sure he knew where he had to go.

I didn't explain my wet hair or why I had on my gym clothes. Or what I had been doing. I did feel better by Richard's anger and desire to get our stuff back. After the lengthy phone conversation and explanation, I felt overly tired. I told Richard I had made a bed for myself in the living room. I would see him in the morning.

Our house didn't have a standard overhead light in the living room. Closing the entrance door from the kitchen, I observed as I came through the unlit dining room a pale light trail, this light was unfamiliar to me. As I took steps further toward the living room, the light revealed it was coming from our neighbor's second floor bedroom. Their light filtered through one of our smaller living room windows and its beam shone on my made-up bed on the floor. First, I was ashamed the neighbors would see the bed made up on the floor. Then, the closed off aloneness I had felt when first entering the dining room subsided. The light shining mid-stream showed dust particles, a vivid reminder of the pixie dust from Tinker-bell and the story of Peter Pan. I started humming to myself. I was no longer afraid. I knew then I would never be returning to my previous way of life. Pixie-dust light had reminded me, no more childhood imagination. I hadn't realized until now, but I had made the choice to not live with Mom while swimming back to shore. Little had I known until now, what I had learned looking after my siblings would provide me with valuable support. I lay on my back and tried to think of what could help me. My small skill set included my minimal education. This thought led me to question myself on how can I find a way of earning income now. It seemed to me I wanted to remove my youth entirely to escape these next few years. I took a breath. I was sighing. It was hard to think. What else did I actually have to contribute? My domestic knowledge, along with what was right and wrong. My military upbringing from my dad gave way to my best mannered cordial self. Remembering a British quote, I decided to apply it to myself. I took a deep breath and said to myself, loudly, "Keep your chin up, Beth!" Talking to myself helped me to get to sleep. Turning away from the window and the light, staring at the empty wall, I felt moral determination in defense of Mom being so willful at times. Mom's continued behavior now sealed us from returning to our childhood. I now knew I couldn't truly count on our mom for protection.

Drifting off to sleep, I felt I had to rely on myself. I had begun to be conscious of my reliance while I was swimming back to shore. I was coming away from being a shadow to others. I had been in the shadows of both Mom and Dad as a kid, forced to take on their multiple tasks. I no longer had to put aside my needs to bridge the gap that was necessary in a child-rearing family life. Now, in this empty room with nothing surrounding me, I was struck by the thought. Not of what I had lost, but how much I felt overwhelmed by what may have begun. I hadn't been given any personal life or hobbies, other than occasionally reading. My mom hadn't allowed my friendships to develop. Even Barbara asking me to go to the public library made my mom balk at her invitation. I had been taught early to compete using skills like learning to ride a bike, playing tennis, swimming, or skating. They were learned but rarely practiced. Maybe now, I could further my skills. I reflected on the idea that my mom had been intending on grooming me for a career, and leaving home through marriage. Luckily, no images came to my mind regarding those ideas. Most of what I had learned from my mom's regime could be copied to such an extent both Richard and I could manage our daily lives.

Feeling betrayed, paralyzed by fear with daily unfamiliarity and minimal support, the previous week, I now feel that I am becoming trusting with my aloneness in my new beginnings. It was now easier to replace whom I could be loyal to. This would free me from blaming myself. I no longer felt I had to use reminders of cruelty or past experiences to defend my actions. These further events increased the divide between us. The minimal steps in place to live here now helped stop me from further doubting my actions. My new actions would encourage my self-preservation. I had lived so many of these daily routines already.

I now realized that the swimming toward ending my life was a misunderstanding of my fear. I was more frightened by being given a chance to do what I would need for my life to open up in a way that, so far, was truly unfamiliar to me. I did not know yet what that would or could be.

If I could take a breath, I could maybe relax a little with the uncertainty. Maybe I could make living in the house feel like I belonged here. Living with my folks, the house itself had never felt safe to me as a child. I had no choice as a child with what to do with my feelings of aloneness and the feelings of living in isolation with my family. Clearly, with no telltale signs of personal objects as reminders. No bed, the only lights being overhead ceiling lights, the empty closets, no living room furniture, no kitchen table or chairs. All the past gone. The hollowness gave me a new determining resolve and a new space for decisiveness. The furnishings had never lent themselves to my feeling cozy at home. I didn't feel a loss or a missing connection to these new vacant surroundings. The empty space and the obvious shelter the house provided this past week had a different feeling. A safety like I had never felt before. Now the challenge was how to make this new way of living acceptable, to myself first, then our peers, and neighbors around us.

Chapter 15

In the morning before the arrival of our relatives, I toured the house. I allowed myself to stretch, to feel the expansion of the house and what warmth it could provide for me. The shutting of the doors to hide away the emptiness wasn't a concern for me. Well, not while in our own privacy. My bedroom, which I had hoped would have provided a refuge for me, was in fact now the entire house. For once, the sunbeam coming through the small living room windows without curtains made me happy. Thank goodness, Mom had left the venetian blinds on both the front windows of the house and the dining room windows. I was beginning to appreciate what we had. Would my aunt and uncle understand what we had?

Both Richard and I had taken care of the household chores for many years and now had our new adapted system in place. My brother still had his bed and clothing but I was not sure what I was going to be wearing daily. While I was waiting, I went outside to the backyard and surveyed any possibility of the trees giving fruit.

At the top of the plum tree, totally unattainable without a ladder, were a few plums but they were looking old and bruised. The apple tree near the neighboring yard was loaded with apples that were small and tart in flavor. I didn't care. I simply had had enough toast, jam, and peanut butter. Stomachache or neighbors watching, I needed a change in my diet. I moved closer to the apple tree near the adjoining fence. What could possibly scare me now?

Chapter 16

It was barely 11 a.m. when Alan came over. The early morning silence felt like I had been up for hours. Richard as well. I had bathed and hand-washed both my pants and shirt from last night. I hung my clothing on the outside clothesline to dry. I hoped they would dry before my relatives arrived. Having to continue to wear my gym clothes was embarrassing. Richard and I cleaned up the house, he vacuumed and I washed down the bathroom. Now, while I was finishing up with daily chores, I watched Alan yawning. He gave me the impression he still hadn't had enough sleep. We were asking him to help us bring back our stuff in his truck, Richard's dresser, my bed, and clothing. I suspected it had to be an awkward position to be in. Alan was wearing his heavy plaid shirt, his framed body weight looking older than his just sixteen years. He gave me a quiet smile while standing there, leaning against the kitchen cupboards. His posture reflected a rounding of his shoulders, he had one leg crossed over the other and was wearing his sand-colored desert laced up shoes. He waited patiently for Richard to finish up in the bathroom. I realized he had a gentle nature. He seemed very different from my brother right now.

Richard abruptly entered the room and told us his plan. Richard spoke, looking at Alan and away from me, "Beth you must stay behind with our aunt and uncle. We don't know how Mom will react to you being there." I looked over and saw Alan wasn't sure what Richard was trying to convey. Richard continued by saying he, Kate, and Alan would storm our mom's new house to re-gain our belongings. I realized that I was asking for my brother's help. I needed my belongings. I now felt how I was coming to my own decision to not live with Mom. I had more at risk than Richard. Richard finished up by saying and grinning at Alan, "This plan may be easier said than done." Richard's plan, no matter how it played out, was a further step to protecting what we had begun.

Kate was onboard when she arrived, and of course Aunt Mabel was a little anxious, as my mom was her sister. What was great is they brought with them, on the ferry, a cardboard table. Also, paper plates and cutlery. They planned spaghetti and a salad with French bread. I had never tasted spaghetti, lettuce salad, or garlic French bread before. I was very distracted by all of this because food, up to now, had been repetitive to say the least.

When Richard, Alan, and Kate were well on their way. Aunt Mabel and I were in conversation with our Uncle Walter with their tales. They loved spending time at their cabin located outside of Victoria, off the Malahat Highway near Mill Bay. They had just recently heard the news of our plight when returning to Vancouver where they lived and worked. I watched as my aunt's expression, once her tale had been recounted, returned to concern for us with a repeating look of anxiousness. If I took notice with eye contact, she immediately changed her frowned expression to a smile and nervous giggle. We had made both the salad and spaghetti, when Richard, Kate, and Alan were back. It seemed incredibly short in time since their departure from us. I quickly checked our clothesline. My clothes from the night before were stiff-cold to handle but wind-dry. I quickly retreated into our bathroom and changed as I heard loud furniture movements ascending upstairs.

Chapter 17

Alan and Richard brought back my bed and the bedding for my bed. I felt subdued by their actions, yet appreciative. Richard had his dresser but because of his anger, he brought an extra drawer from our mom's dresser. He had probably intended revenge. Richard's tone reflected his threat to Mom. Richard yelled at us of how he had spoken to our mom. "Do not come back and take our stuff again." My feelings surprised me but I had immediate regret for his action on my behalf, as the missing drawer would be a daily visual reminder for her. Mom claimed that my clothing had been sold and since our siblings were in tears with the abrupt disruption, Richard didn't feel he could press to look for my clothing. This is how my brother put it to us over our meal together. Interestingly, my mom's anger wouldn't allow her to negotiate my clothing for her drawer. So much anger allowed me to understand that being here was my safest choice. No one noticed or mentioned anything about having to stand and eat. Kate was standing up, cornered between the kitchen counter and the windowsill with her legs straddled to balance herself with her plate of food. Kate's expression was of annoyance with Richard and his comment, almost sputtering on her words, "Richard, remember it had been difficult with Thomas and Amy watching us as we removed those specific items." Richard and I hadn't, since living alone together, spoken about the absence of our siblings. I can see how my sister found what they just did hadn't been easy for Kate.

Kate, then turned to me and said, "Beth, I will stay an extra day in Victoria and buy you a winter coat."

"Wow," I replied, that felt encouraging. We all ate our dinner. It was remarkable how Alan stayed and joined us. He had always shown himself to me as being incredibly shy. I made the remark, "Alan, your eyes appear to me as if they are literally popping out of your head." Alan's fair-skinned face immediately showed a deep red blushing and in response put his head down, and then looked up grinning. He started laughing and said, "Did we actually just do all of that?"

Richard still was angry but he laughed as well. He spoke in a harsh tone, "We are not going to live with Mom." I agreed by smiling wholeheartedly, forgetting I had my two teeth missing. Seeing my toothless smile, Kate confirmed the time and place for this coming week's appointment for my new appliance with the two teeth. She also told me how to get there.

My aunt and uncle, not remarking on Richard's comment, had retreated outside on the deck for a cigarette break. Kate joined them. The little I overheard in their conversation reflected badly on our dad's absence. Nevertheless, the shared meal between my aunt, uncle, and Kate was enjoyed.

My aunt helped with the few utensils that needed washing. Her frown was back. I noticed it while wiping down the stove. She was noticing my bare feet as we walked through the hallway toward the front door. I took in her lingering, while she viewed the empty rooms. She gave me a kind farewell. The house was empty again. I happily cleared up any remaining mess and then went upstairs to make up my own bed in my room. Afterwards, I lay down again, trying to make peace with the aloneness and thought, *Really? Is that all I can expect from my relatives?*

Chapter 18

Lying on my bed, I started to reflect on how Richard and I had this new beginning come about. It had started so long before our time. My mother was born in a small town, Swift Current in the Province, Saskatchewan. Her dad had been a homesteader, relocating from Suffolk, England in the late 1800s. He later became a gentleman rancher because he had established sources of income not dependent on his ranching. My grandfather's ranch was located just outside Maple Creek, Saskatchewan. My grandmother had grown up in Maple Creek and became a nurse. She had met my grandfather when he was considerably older. They married, and when my mom turned fifteen, he suddenly died from a heart attack. This was a big shock and with this grief still fresh, my mom set herself a goal to finish her high school year. She then left home to live with relatives of her father's in Seattle, Washington, United States. While living with her relatives, she also received financial support to attend secretarial school. My mom's first secretarial employment came with having to move across the country to Washington D.C. My mom successfully relocated and worked for the Australian Embassy. My mom became a socialite and while attending the embassy parties, met my dad. He gave her the impression. This was how he enjoyed life. This life they shared so happily, continued for a length of time. My dad was born in Canterbury, England. He had a daughter from a previous marriage (my stepsister Kate) and expressed he had no interest in having more children. Dad's first wife was killed during the Second World War while living in England. After this tragic loss of Kate's mother, both sets of grandmothers shared bringing up Kate. My dad was then left free to pursue his career. After the war, he was stationed through the British forces to work in Washington DC, USA. My mother's story to us was she had been assessed by her physician and told she couldn't physically carry any children, before she married my dad. She felt confident they would continue as they were, enjoying the life they enjoyed so heartily. Their firstborn, a surprise, was Richard. Being a son, he was accepted. I knew this was true, by the telling of the string of names given to my brother at birth by my dad. My mom had been proud of giving dad a son. My folks moved to England. Several additional months later, I was born in a British Royal Air Force (RAF) base hospital. My mother described at times to me, in a way a young girl might have understood, how she had difficulty accepting her new life. Living a quiet life in England without parties. A few years later after my grandmother came for a visit, my mom soon after took the initiative to return alone, with us to live in Canada. I later would understand my mother had inherited some monies from her stepbrothers through the sale of her father's ranchland to spur her move.

When my mother shared her most beloved stories, they mostly reflected how she had enjoyed parties. Living with girlfriends, she never learned to cook and had no interest in doing so. My mom said she had shared her duties by being the cleaner of their apartment. Not learning to cook past basic skills carried on into her married life. My mom failed to share with me her deeper reasons for her continued impertinence, wanting to afford a lifestyle she had enjoyed in Washington D.C. It never occurred to me, how her determination to live a larger life was related to having been brought up on a successful ranch outside a small town. Her father had been well respected for his contributions to the town of Maple Creek. He had been a part of the first ranchers and farmers to invest in shipping wheat out of Swift Current to other parts of the country by train. My mother actively pursued choices, distinguishing and believing she was different because of her early influences growing up. My mom used instead, her young adult newly acquired experiences to spread her wings and form her new life. We moved to Oak Bay, having lived in a less expensive area in Esquimalt, Victoria. We had started going to private school before attending a public school in Oak Bay, which was better in her opinion. Mom was adamant in not volunteering in our school because she believed it would result in bickering over small unnecessary matters. Her demands on us may have been furthered pushed, knowing her mother-in-law had been brought up in a small northern town outside Blackpool, England. After my dad's mother and father married, they moved south to Canterbury, England. My dad's mother changed her English dialect to fit into the new larger community, which was not an easy task. I had been told my grandmother had a very strong northern accent. It would have taken commitment to change her accent. At the same time, she went on to learn how to play tennis to further fit in her husband's community in the south of England. My mother's need to also socially climb placed, perhaps, unnecessary financial burden onto us. My mother's desires along with her past were not fully appreciated by my dad as he had his own shortcomings. My dad had himself been brought up in a larger privileged community, along with being his mother's favorite son. Because of this favoritism, he did not learn any real practical life skills while living at home. At the age of fifteen, without permission from his folks, he was assisted with funds from his aunt to pursue becoming an airplane pilot. My dad's resentment of his dad not sending him to the best schools would haunt him into his early adult life. It may have spurred his rebellious persistence in becoming a pilot. Not being placed in particular schools, directly impacted your promotions in the British Military Forces. When he ventured into the Second World War, he came with a practiced skill. My dad's practiced skill from an early age awarded him becoming a Wing Commander Officer at the young age of 26 in the Royal Air Force for Britain. His newly acquired position came with an assigned batman. The position of a batman is a personal servant assigned to assist an officer with tasks and duties in line with the officer's duties. These duties asked of my dad often, I was led to believe with poke in fun humor extended beyond my dad's military requirement needs. After I was born and once my mother had returned to Canada, my dad's next assignment as an officer was to be an appointment in Japan. My dad made the choice to retire from the RAF and to come to Canada instead, where his current family resided.

My mother had, by this time, settled down working as a secretary and a bookkeeper for a successful local sawmill company in Victoria. Although, I suspect that my dad struggled with his new arrangement being home with us kids and trying to win Mom over again. Contacts led him to pursue becoming a Social Welfare civil servant. Becoming a civil government employee worked well with his background. Unfortunately, his non-practical skills, living without hired help of a housekeeper and nanny was of little practical help to his wife and children. Both my mom and dad longed for their earlier days for different reasons perhaps. But what had never been truly accepted between them became my mother's focus in anger and disappointment with her choices. She was unfulfilled with her husband and current social achievements. In the earlier days in our house, our mom and dad would have parties and monthly bridge nights, recreating their social lives together. Mom wanted to continue to strategize a larger social life in Victoria with Dad. Any lessons we were taught, such as tennis, were learned while belonging to a club giving her access to new expansion for her social needs. In the meantime, we were taught all housekeeping chores, including cleaning the oven and defrosting the fridge from an early age. My brother and I had to boil water on the stove and lift the pot from the stove and place it in the icebox. All of this, I learned by the age of five from my brother, and practiced soon after. I actually would get inside the oven to reach and clean the back wall of the oven. Very Hansel and Gretel like, the cleaner burnt my hands, as there were no gloves small enough to fit me. An all-day job left to us, while my mother went out and shopped and had her weekly hair appointment. My mother's demands did not include demonstrating she either cared for us or loved us. Her fits of anger worsened with two more additional children. Then, when my half-sister moved to

Canada after finishing school in England, Mom couldn't imagine her life would be defined as anything other than domesticity. The same belief my dad most hated, having to entertain for himself. Certainly, during the fifties and early sixties, this was a plight for those who had lived with awarded recognition through their personal ambitions boosted by events during the Second World War. I believe my folk's nature was reconciled by their accomplishments temporarily after the war. By physically removing themselves from their past painful childhood experiences, the war behind them and locating in a scenic provincial town in Canada, they had the opportunity to redefine life on different terms. Not entirely embraced, Dad hid his fatherhood by seeking new recognition through belonging to both sailing and gliding clubs. Mom did the same by having bridge parties and continuing to push herself to live a similar socially expanded lifestyle she had once enjoyed as a young adult.

Both our folks in their domestic neglect, opened the path for how Richard and I were prepared to be self-sufficient before ever living on our own. We were tired of my mother's continued anger and unrealistic expectations. By not leaving and living with Mom, and knowing Dad wanted to keep the house, we were able to engage him into supporting us financially. He could decide his own terms of how much minimal support he would give us instead of being directed by the family court. Also, living away from us first in Victoria and later moving to the mainland, he didn't have to offer us emotional or fatherly guidance. Dad had drilled into us from a very young age, he would only respond to our questions for help if it included a forthcoming solution.

Chapter 19

The next day was Sunday. My girlfriend was required to go to church with her family, so I waited until the middle of the afternoon before calling her on our telephone.

I was going to have to tell her what my life was at the moment because I needed to borrow clothes to wear to school. Barbara and I had shared clothes all through grade seven. Her mom made all of Barbara's clothes and probably made new ones for the fall. I felt Barbara wouldn't mind sharing some of her older clothing.

I had hand-washed my underwear and pressed the clothes I had for Monday just in case, I had to wear what I had worn on Friday again. I had found an old summer dress in the back of my closet, so I had prepared that as well. Hanging the newly hand-washed marmalade-colored dress to dry. I was enjoying how the dress had both a white and silver colored glitter thread throughout the patterned cotton material. It made me feel and remember a happier time as the glitter thread reflected brightly in the sun-filled bathroom. I wondered why it had been left. These very vivid moments in memory relieved the boredom of too much time on my hands.

As a rule, when Barbara and I met after dinner, we met at twilight at the corner. I had told Barbara I had some news and it might take a little time to tell her about what was going on. Barbara agreed not to bring her puppy, (a beagle) a possible distraction, and we could just maybe walk around the block.

Of course, I was anxious as I told my brother, I was going to meet Barbara. Giving him my reason, he wished me good luck. Barbara was eager to hear what I had called for, yet I noticed she was impatient as her mom wanted her home promptly as it was an evening before beginning a school day.

Barbara described her day as having been the usual Sunday, church and family dinner. I told her that I had been meaning to tell her that my mom and dad had left. Barbara said, "What do you mean they left?" I took a deep breath. It wasn't easy to tell someone you were living alone in a five-bedroom house by yourself with your brother. I wanted to tell her the minimal amount as the whole no-furniture thing still felt odd to me to have to explain. The daily reminder of the house continuing to sound like an echoing building when you walked through or if you spoke, still felt eerie at times.

Barbara listened attentively, taking her time. Then she replied in a witless tone, "When will they be back?"

I was taken aback by this remark and answered, "Ah, I wasn't sure." At that moment, I felt judged and to continue with my explanation and asking for help I was seeking, was difficult. I rushed my words to tell Barbara the following, "My mom is mad that I haven't gone to live with her and I chose to live with my brother and dad, even though my dad wasn't here either at the moment." I then said, "My mom was so mad she had returned on Friday to take all my clothes. I only had what I was wearing on Friday and an old summer worn-out dress, short in length but okay, I guess." I can't imagine what my tone was like in that moment saying all of this to her. Barbara's clear blue eyes appeared wide-eyed. Barbara, when nervous, scratched her nose and swept her hand across her forehead to adjust her bangs.

Barbara offered right away to bring up clothes for me to wear. She went into skirt descriptions of ones she felt were longer in length for me, and what went with my style. Just listening to her made my life easier in that moment. I sighed in relief. Thank god, she was my friend. Since Barbara and I walked to school together in the mornings, she first offered to bring a cardigan to wear so I wouldn't be too cold wearing the short summer dress. Then, she offered to come up tomorrow after school and bring me something else to wear.

We didn't hug but my god, I could have hugged her for a long time, this was real help. The streetlights were just coming on when I ran all the way home to tell Richard.

Chapter 20

When I returned, I told Richard it went okay, he was happy for me I could tell as he smiled. He then said Kate had called and explained why she hadn't come today, and why she couldn't come tomorrow, and she would be in touch later in the month to buy me a coat.

I would now be hoping the warmth of summer days would last awhile yet. The following day, Barbara remembered her cardigan for me to wear to school. I was so grateful for her help. Not having any change of clothes to wear would have been extremely noticeable at school. I was ready with my homework. Homework had gone easier after meeting with her last evening, so I was prepared for the week. The only thing was I had to come home each day at lunchtime. I didn't yet know how to bring my sandwich. I didn't have anything to carry it in or have the opportunity to buy wax paper. I had to remember to remind Richard.

The morning classes completed without duress. I felt better coming back from school and having lunch at home. Richard too, had come home and brought his friend, Stephen. Stephen was astonished with how we were living and remarked on how lucky we were. That wasn't something I expected. But I knew from my more recent conversations with my brother, how Stephen was known for being outspoken. Still, his outspoken bluntness was no more than embarrassing for me today. Continuing to listen to Stephen and waiting for the bread for my sandwich to toast I thought theoretically, philosophically, (Stephen's words, not mine) *Yes, it was okay,* but to see it each day not changing for the better, was difficult. I was beginning to feel a different kind of burden was upon us. Living our life secretly was one thing, going public was another.

After school, Barbara walked back home with me, which was unusual as she had a boyfriend and they usually hung out together after school. But I think she was curious and so she came back to our house. I, of course, immediately forgot we didn't have a stick of living room furniture except for the cardboard table. It was such a novelty for me to have anyone over. The cardboard table was set up in the kitchen. Luckily, the door to the living room was closed when we came in the front door. The echo sound was muted as we walked the length of the hallway as the bedroom doors were closed as well. We walked to the back of the house and through the entrance to the kitchen. Barbara's first remark was why hadn't I locked the front door. I couldn't reply without laughing. *Really, what else could honestly be taken?*

Barbara asked, "Can I come upstairs?"

I answered, "Of course." Maybe she wanted to check and see if I really didn't have any clothes and since I kept my closet doors wide open, it was easy for her to see it was true. Barbara, then said she would meet me at the corner again tonight and I could borrow clothes.

On our way back downstairs to the main floor, she asked nonchalantly, "Beth, what are you planning to do with your vanity table?"

It wasn't a priority so I just went on to say, "Barbara, I am excited how my sister is planning on buying me a winter coat."

My tone in my reply was probably unnecessary, for Barbara stopped talking for a minute. Then at the bottom of the stairs she remarked, "That would be good." I hadn't meant to cut off answering Barbara's question of my beginnings of a vanity table. It was difficult for me who hadn't any basic clothing to wear to comprehend what would have interested her to ask what I would do next with the vanity table. Her interest surprised me at the same time. As she had offered her opinion on it another time and I had tried to explain to her then how my mother wasn't able to figure out what to do with it either. Barbara's mom would have made a skirt from fabric for it, simple and effective. My mom would take years to figure out what could be done with it outside of throwing it away. Our mothers were as different as night and day.

I think at this point, Barbara didn't know what else to say to me. What are you making for dinner isn't usually asked by your twelve-year-old girlfriend? Again, I thanked her for helping me and told her if I did get new clothes, she was welcome to share them. When she left, I missed her terribly. The moment of comfort was over.

That night, Richard and I ate the left-over spaghetti and salad. Richard then said Alan was going to take him to the laundry mat and grocery store. I was happy but not too excited as my brother always bought the same stuff to eat. *Wax paper please!* Then a quick visit with Barbara at the corner to borrow clothes added further appreciation to my day.

Chapter 21

The next day, Barbara asked me on the way to school if I wanted to come to her house for dinner. Yes, I wanted to come for dinner, are you kidding me!

Since Richard ate and bought what he liked, I didn't feel badly going out for dinner. Barbara mentioned we could go through her clothes and find outfits for me to wear at the same time.

That evening on arrival at Barbara's, the aroma of home cooking was overwhelming to me. We first met Mrs. Winston in the hallway entrance. She was a person who I felt was kind, yet reserved. I wanted to thank her right away for having me over for dinner but I couldn't get her to look me in the eye, so I remained quiet and polite. She could see I was wearing clothes I had borrowed from Barbara. I felt a little embarrassed, another time having to go public with my situation. Barbara and I ate homemade baked cookies in the den on their new couch and watched *American Bandstand. American Bandstand* was a show for teens to watch. They had the newest recorded songs sung by the pop star musicians. Kids on the show danced and the audience learned popular new dance steps. I hadn't even recognized, how we didn't have a T. V. anymore.

When Barbara's dad came home, we were all called for dinner. I began to feel uncomfortable on my way to the kitchen. Barbara's older sister, Rachael, and her brother, Bruce, were already seated in the kitchen nook. Alice, Barbara's youngest sister, sat in a high chair. Rachael had set the dinner table for us. Sitting down, it felt amazing to be a part of a family. I could feel my spirits lift. Belonging somewhere for just this meal, felt amazing.

The meal contained frozen vegetables like Richard had bought, a casserole I had never seen or tasted before. Until then I hadn't even heard the word 'casserole' before. It was only when I was asked to pass the casserole, I knew what it was. The casserole was made with noodles and tuna. My thought turned to how my mom didn't know how to put food together in a dish and baked it in the oven. My mom had continued to resist using a recipe to learn to make something new to eat. My mom had told me many times over and over she hadn't any interest in learning how to cook. The consequences of her behavior allowed me to both enjoy this meal and become self-sufficient, having learned how to cook. I believe Mrs. Winston's simple-to-make dinner was a message of what I too might be able to prepare for dinner. I didn't get the message at that time.

Barbara's dad made a joke at Rachael's expense. Rachael was not impressed and so the tone was set. No one mentioned why I was invited in the middle of the week. I had only to answer one question about school. During a moment of silence, Barbara mentioned I had been voted into the position of student president representative for my class again. While the dessert was being served to us, Bruce was already fighting to not have to help with the dishes. I was quick to get up and do the dishes. Rachael washing, myself drying, and Barbara putting the dishes away. I liked Rachael's ease and speed with what had to be done with clearing the dishes and washing them. I saw in her, a basic happy teenager.

Then without eye contact or recognition from Mrs. Winston, I thanked her for dinner. Then, Barbara took me up to the room she shared with Rachael. I was embarrassed at first with Rachael's presence, along with her poignant, intended stare. But, almost immediately, there was a phone call for Rachael and she left the bedroom. When Barbara took out clothes from last year, I recognized them right away. I began to relax. She told me her mom had actually lengthened a couple of the skirts for me to wear. I could not have asked for a better friend or gift. I made a point of going back to the kitchen when we returned to the main floor before leaving to thank Mrs. Winston once again.

Chapter 22

The next evening, I had just finished my dinner with Richard and was on my way to do my homework. Richard spoke up, "Beth, could we do the dishes together and talk about rules we might need while we are living on our own."

After the time spent at Barbara's house, I can see how difficult our situation is for everyone. Each neighboring person must have thought it would resolve itself shortly. Perhaps, if we continued to keep our place in order, along with good behavior we would lessen the chance of anyone interfering with our decision. It wouldn't have been so difficult to explain if our dad lived with us, but he didn't. I hadn't even inquired yet where in fact our dad was living? Richard didn't tease me about my teeth anymore. He didn't try to bully me in the same way as when we lived with our mom and dad, and our siblings. I answered, "Sure."

Richard's first rule was we could have liquor in the house but no drugs. At that moment in time, I thought about this and decided he must mean no aspirin when it came to drugs. I was drying the dishes and looked down at the counter and not at Richard. This idea of concern about drugs was new to me. Second rule, I was to tell him if I could, what I was up to, if I had a plan to go out. I thought about how I had tried to drown myself last week and was glad I didn't have to report on that. So, in that moment, deciding not to reveal to my brother what I had done, my heart was further broken with yet another secret. I couldn't see myself telling anyone how I ventured forth through two potential deaths of myself trying to make sense of my personal experience of being abandoned by our mom. By not telling, I was sealing off, in my mind, our illusions of previous misery. I was lumping both my brother's experience and my own as the same. I couldn't see them as separate and behaved as he did by not allowing my feelings to show. This was moving me toward feeling I was on my own when unrealistic expectations were made of me. My brother was here with practical support but I wasn't able to ask to be comforted. If anything, I felt like I had to step it up with more skills. Even if at this time I felt disappointed by others choices. These were the costs to making this new life work. Thus, I began shaping my first known character flaw. Perceiving I was on my own when having to find solutions. Third rule, now I was in grade eight, I might be asked out on a date. I had dated a little last year in grade seven but mostly just watching a movie in the middle of the day and going for a walk. A couple of times, I had been asked to go skating in a group, or a house party. My mom hadn't given me any rules about dating. I had just found out what was acceptable for my age through friendships and what I saw in either public places or private parties. Once, my mom had told me not to accept a cigarette from a stranger. I suspected there was more to that idea than she was suggesting at the time.

Richard pointed out he didn't think it would be a good idea if I had a boyfriend living alone. Living alone. Those words had me shivering, I hardly got the gist of what my brother said next. I had to believe I could make this work. He went on to say, "It might give him ideas in taking advantage of you."

I couldn't see myself with a boyfriend. I said, "I will limit my dating to one person, only three dates, and then not see the boy anymore." I remember feeling confident in my answer. I did later go to bed reflecting on how Richard's comment re-someone taking advantage of me. Did this mean I couldn't count on Richard's support in this matter? I was reminded of what Stephen had told me. Richard's friends were off my list of ever to date. I guess this is how he is looking out for me.

Fourth rule mentioned was we cleaned the house every Saturday morning, no matter what. We would figure out how much the weekly cost at the laundry mat would be and give our dad the information. We also needed Dad to support us by having an account at the confectionary store. We needed a place where we could buy milk, bread, and any essential item we might need either for school or ourselves. (I was going to need Kotex pads pretty soon for my menstrual periods.)

Richard had already spoken to Dad on the phone about this idea of having an account at the corner store. Richard had worked in the summer and was probably not happy to have to buy food until Dad came up with the funds. Dad hadn't come to stay or see us. It had been over ten days already. Definitely Richard's experience in Ontario this past summer was helping him cope with our situation here at the moment. It did help me so much how determined he was in making this chosen life together work.

Chapter 23

The next day, without notice, Dad brought us approximately thirty loaves of white sliced bread, a new tin of strawberry jam, and a new tin of peanut butter. Dad also included a tub of margarine, along with a zillion-bananas. How the heck were we to eat all of those. Dad had come at lunchtime and seen how we had friends eating our food. I could see our dad was surprised. Later that evening while we were preparing for dinner, Dad dropped by. He was intent on directing his conversation to Richard. Dad said, "I was impressed you were having friends back to the house at lunchtime." He asked, "Richard, how many friends are coming?"

Richard answered, "I am not sure, Dad."

Dad then said, "I could support this idea if you kept it up Richard." This was my dad, always showing concern for others rather than his actual family members. Even though we may have felt somewhat appreciative. Richard's posture showed me his agitation with our dad's comment.

Instead of lashing out, he took offence with Dad's purchasing margarine instead of butter. Richard remarked in a harsh tone, "Dad, we don't eat margarine."

Dad laughed. He had just placed the margarine in the fridge and while his back was facing us, Richard was adamantly shaking his head. "Richard, margarine has vitamin E added into it." Richard then promptly left the room. This seems funny to mention but we had been doing everything ourselves for almost two weeks by now. I guess we weren't sure we could trust his help. Dad had laid all the food along a wall in the kitchen we had left it there. Dad left without another word being spoken. Richard returned a little later to help with dinner. Richard and I picked up some of the food and put it in our cupboards and left the rest as our dad had placed them. Richard was probably happy Dad would provide this extra lunchtime food but he wasn't going to thank him.

Slowly, I was becoming aware more friends of Richard's and one or two of mine were coming for lunch regularly. An informal invitation to our friends to come at lunchtime ignites interest as anyone who comes could eat our sandwiches of peanut butter, jam, and the new addition, tuna with mayonnaise.

Coming home for lunch and meeting Richard's friends, was interesting for sure. We often sat outside together on the surface of our deck while the weather remained mild. One blond-haired guy was preparing his sandwich for lunch on our cardboard table. At the same time, talking about how his mother was on welfare and couldn't afford to feed him lunch. Then with a big smile, said, "This was perfect to be able to come here." Since my dad was a social worker himself, I found his comment uncomfortable. At the same time, why was I uncomfortable? Why couldn't his mom feed him lunch? More importantly, why didn't he care that we knew.

Right away, Richard offered him our margarine. The guy laughed. But said if we meant it, he would gladly take it. Seeing him pack it off with him when he left that day seemed surprising to me, that we were able to give something to help someone else. Stephen, of course, came regularly to our lunches, the others were new to me. Stephen was the philosopher and always wanted to talk about the different ways man defended his right for the need for war. The Cuban Crisis had been on the agenda today. Stephen, although in high school, was involved in knowing the ways of politics.

My civic duty with being a class president representative was a joke to him. I wasn't offended. I wasn't trying to change the world. I was trying to fit in it. I had also succeeded in getting to my dentist appointment to get my new mold taken for my appliance to be formed and my two false teeth to be attached. I would be smiling again soon.

Chapter 24

October was feeling frosty to me. A cold evening was indeed a cold evening at home. Without heat being provided, the emptiness from no warmth in furnishings added a further surrounding of coldness. The food choices remained limited. The struggle of living with intolerance amongst family members had subsided but the reality left me having to face the grimness, each day alone. My brother continued to be rarely home or locked away studying in his room. Richard had a great way of focusing his anger in a direction that would help him to succeed. He had thought nothing of taking our card table and making it a desk for himself.

I did though enjoy the informal gathering lunchtime friendships offered. I had fun with simple pleasures enjoying the beach and walking more frequently, occasionally with a friend, Barbara or Janet. I now had time to listen to my friends and acquaintances. My mind was completely opening to new ideas and experiences in those first few weeks. Recently, a neighbor's daughter, who had helped get me to learn how to skate, called out to me when I was walking home one day from school. Jane was quite a bit older. I didn't know if Mom was keeping in touch with her mom or not. She said she had a pair of size eight figure skates and wanted to know if I could use them. I was at least a size seven and a half. I said, "Sure." As I walked toward her lawn, she went inside to fetch them. She then handed them to me quickly from the front doorstep landing, saying, "Sorry, I'm in a hurry." I smiled, thanked her and left. It felt abrupt but I was still grateful.

Our lives were changing. I began to read more. My thirteenth birthday came and went.

Kate announced she would soon be on her way and we would be shopping for a coat for me in no time. Kate, didn't come and sleep at the house but rather turned up in a cab one Saturday. I was over the moon to see Kate, so was Richard. Kate and I hopped on the bus at the end of our street. The bus took us downtown to Victoria's city center. Arriving at Douglas street we walked along the main street until women's dress shops, came into view. I felt the crispness in the air. The sun, luckily, was shining brightly, giving some warmth to the end of the month October day. The shop we entered was located near the Hudson's Bay Company department store.

I had never been in a women's wear clothing store before in my life. My mother enjoyed shopping for herself. But never took us shopping unless we were going specifically to the children's wear store. The number of coats looked amazing and I could care less, which one was chosen. A brand-new coat was a lot for me to receive at this time.

I don't remember trying on many coats but as soon as I tried on this royal blue coat, I remember Kate saying, "That's the one we want!" The wool coat was double breasted with silver metal buttons even on the shoulders, giving it a distinct military look. It had its own scarf made of the same material and the coat was fully lined in length and I could smell the newness. "How wonderful," I said to Kate. I couldn't thank Kate enough.

Kate, I believe, spent a great deal of money on this garment. The in-style design along with it being wool, made it more expensive.

Afterwards, we sat and had a coke somewhere nearby and she told me how she had set up these coupons for me to shop at the department store Woodward's and how I could buy up to $25.00 a month in clothing. This would mean I could buy underwear and socks, and maybe a pair of penny loafers. This was truly a reconciled moment between us. Kate had time perhaps to have thought how she had influenced our events as well. The extra money did allow me to feel hope. I was thankful. While, drinking our cokes, I did ask Kate what she could do more for our situation. Kate didn't answer. She just held her hand over her chin firmly and with her elbow on the table, sighed understandingly. Then taking her other hand, looking down into her drink, moved her straw around the ice in a circular motion. I saw for once she had removed her brightly required nail polish for her position as an airline stewardess. I noted how it left markings permanently, staining her nails. It was an indicator to me that her life was hectic and not always easy either. Taking the time to come and do this act of kindness was a reminder to me to go back thanking her for her help with both the coat and gift coupons. Kate herself at this time was just twenty-two years old. I also had picked up my appliance and it was fitting nicely in my mouth and the adjustment period had been pretty smooth overall. I could now smile at her with delight.

Chapter 25

When we returned home, we found out Dad was visiting in Victoria, as well this particular Saturday. The four of us were standing in the kitchen together, a rare treat. As soon as the usual compliments over the coat were made, Dad was explaining how Richard and I might need to go to court as our mom wanted more money for child support. I started to cry and my brother turned his head directly at me and shouted, "Don't ever cry again, it will never help." Richard the bully again with his harsh tone affected me immediately. "What about how she treated me before she left?" I spoke out. No eye contact from anyone or answer to my question. I noticed in that moment as I said those words out loud watching for a reaction from Dad, Richard, and Kate. No reaction. In that close proximately, not one of them seeing the stress it may have had on me or continued to have on me. Now that was worrisome for me. Richard immediately left the room. I felt that Richard, although frustrated, in having to argue most things to get our dad to pay for us to stay in the house continued to not want to live with Mom any longer either. But his tone did not indicate I was safe in relying on his continued support. Richard was my only witness to the incident with Mom, but I didn't trust he would go out of his way to help me further. I could not argue to stay with Dad. I was not yet fourteen. I could officially be told by the courts to live with my mom. I removed myself from the room as Dad did his usual pacing when anxious with a decision to be made. The joke us kids had on our dad was whenever he had a practical concern since he had left the British forces and had to give up his beloved batman. Every required daily living decision was overwhelming to him. Whether a light bulb needed changing or the right coinage to wash clothes in a laundry mat. Making a stand for us was well beyond him on most occasions.

Also, not one thought to console me either, my Aunt Mabel and Uncle Walter now that I remembered their reaction to me had been the same. No one would acknowledge I had a difficult moment with our mom. Would acknowledging her behavior mean the need for an adult to take responsibility? Would the turn of events following that responsibility be worse than our present circumstances? Too embarrassing or what? I was being cemented into the idea I had to keep further secrets when I was upset. Had I really caused all this by wanting to stay here to go to the same school as my friend and brother? Had telling Richard Mom's secret really allowed her to lash out to such an extent I deserved what I was living without daily support from adult family members? Can no one at least call weekly? Where was Dad living anyhow? I shouted from the living room with agitation in my voice, "Can I, at the very least, visit my brother, Thomas, and sister, Amy?"

Dad remarked, "Beth, that would be impossible in light of having to go to court." He reminded us in a stern tone, "You know very well I am not able to see them either." To be honest, I didn't sympathize with if he saw them or not as he hadn't been around much this past summer to see them anyway.

No one paid attention when I had complained recently as well to the fact Uncle George, my mom's brother, came each Friday night and banged on the garage door repeatedly and for what seemed like longer periods of time, each time. He would yell out something in his drunkenness about how we had to give up and go back to our mom. It did help to remind me to lock the doors, especially the back-basement door. I guess this knocking at the door was a weekly check in.

Chapter 26

Then, one day early in November, I came home on a Friday afternoon to find the entire dining room and kitchen full of furnishings, including paintings. The paintings, although abstract, were astonishingly colorful. I was both bewildered and excited. Richard was taking the time to hang the paintings. The framed paintings included hooks. I yelled out to Richard, "Who gave all this to us and where did it come from?"

Richard explained, "Beth, remember Dad's boss Mr. Simpson, his wife left him once she found out Mom had left Dad. Dad's boss, not needing all the furniture left to him, decided we could use it." We now had a television. We didn't have a couch, but we did have one single living room chair. I was indeed appreciative of my brother in this moment. All our hard work was being accepted! He had led me to believe we could make it alone and here was a very good example of how we were continuing by ourselves. I was indeed grateful.

Dad's boss had a daughter who was eighteen. She kindly passed over to me a whole a vanity with mirror and stool. That was amazing to me. The wood was painted a light pink and mauve. She included a box of clothing, dresses mainly and cardigans. This was entirely unexpected. Although well-worn, I knew how to care for clothing. My mother had made me do the hand wash and iron everyone's clothes in the family at times. Mom had taught me how to mend and how to bring out the newness. In my mother's forgetfulness she had left in the linen closet a small basket containing thread, buttons and needles.

For this as well, I was thankful. My simple domestic skill set was turning out to be more valuable each day. Right away,

I told Barbara. I was glad I had something to offer in return for her generosity. I did learn though by sharing how little I had was difficult at times.

Chapter 27

It was Friday November 22nd. We had just heard over the school's PA system. President John F. Kennedy had been shot. All students were being sent home at noon. President Kennedy had been shot in Dallas, Texas in United States of America, earlier in the day This announcement came before any regular scheduled lunchtime school announcements. It was eight minutes before noon by our clock in the music room. I was being quizzed on sharps, trebles, and notes. I had little interest in this so to me, this was jaw dropping to have a way out of this class early. The seriousness took hold when the announcer told us not to come back to school for the rest of the day. This was completely uncanny and totally unheard of to have an unscheduled day off from school. At first, I could only think how the weather was so hot, not coming back to school was truly great news. The sun shining in the classroom had made it hotter than normal for this time of year, but the teacher had insisted we keep the windows closed. The room was stifling hot with poor air circulation.

Now out on the school ground, this too held much enjoyment. It was overwhelming to take in the seriousness of grieving the potential death of a president presented. Funnily, no one walking out even spoke about what we had just heard. We were shocked with this unexpected event.

We had a T.V. with antennas shaped liked rabbit ears, thanks to Dad's boss. We were settled in the living room watching the day's events unfold as they were released for our viewing. Now with the full realization of what had taken place, it was too awful to think about. The outfit Jacqueline Kennedy, the president's wife, was wearing was the first time I took in further notice of fashion in woman's wear. Even with black and white television, the description of her pink tailored suit was so noticeably in contrast to her bloodied jacket and skirt of her suit. Seeing the perpetrator Lee Harvey Oswald shot and caught on camera seemed staged. As the day wore on, I was exhausted by the repetitiveness of the same coverage. No matter how many times we viewed on television, either Lee Harvey Oswald transferring jails or Jack Ruby shooting Lee Harvey Oswald, it didn't relieve how the overall circumstances would result in any different outcome. President John F. Kennedy died. The worst footage emotionally for me was of Mrs. Jacqueline Kennedy. After she knew something was wrong, she had tried to assist the secret service officer to get into the back of the open Lincoln Continental convertible car. She tried by reaching out with her hand and the officer reaching out at the same time trying to climb onto the trunk of the moving car. Did she realize her husband had been shot? Her quick response to such a horrific moment still astounded me. Her courage was, to me, unprecedented. I had never witnessed such courage by a woman before. As she herself could have been shot. Later, I watched Mrs. Jacqueline Kennedy navigated herself through that horrific day in her pink blood-stained suit. As the T.V. coverage continued over the following days seeing personal touches added to the state funeral held for her husband. Simply by refusing to ride in the larger than life black Cadillac to the burial site. Choosing instead to walk behind the horse drawn casket to her husband's funeral burial. Her leadership and participation reflected her personal strength. How she had asked to light the eternal flame along with her brother-in-law, Robert Kennedy at her husband's gravesite. Instructing her son, 'John-John' to perform his newly practiced salute on the steps of St Matthew Cathedral in front of his father's flag draped coffin. All the while being John-John's actual third birthday. I was witnessing for the first time an act of public influence in woman's leadership. She was opening my mind to how women could take on difficult incorrigible events with grace and honor. Jacqueline Kennedy earned both private and public admiration. I tried to remember a comparative experience in my family's history. My grandmother had definitely taken on leadership qualities once her husband died. With their children still at school, she had to go back to nursing. My grandmother was not able to go back to living on the ranch. My grandfather hadn't made a second will to include his second wife. The ranch went to his first family's children. How humiliating that would have been for my grandmother and her three children to continue to work and live in town. My grandmother went on and continued to help all her children both financially and with much daily help with babysitting for my mom later when needed. Her acts of helping somehow were over shadowed by her own unresolved loss over her husband and home, the ranch. My grandmother was best known to us for her mean side. A side I knew was true but fortunately not practiced on me directly. Had my mom's loss of her cherished father and her home been what contributed to her mean behavior toward us?

The question the next week at lunchtimes was, what was meant by this action of killing a president? The talk amongst my brother and his friends sitting outside on our deck with the sun still warm the following week was, perhaps it had something to do with a conspiracy. I didn't even know the word conspiracy until that moment and what that could honestly mean to us. I don't remember Barbara having any political comment.

Was President Kennedy shot because of leftover concerns with the Cuban Crisis just behind us, or was it because he had been a practicing Catholic? We were only guessing. I didn't even know until then that being a Catholic president was thought as a radical choice for leadership in politics. The possibility of the Mafia behind this never came to mind. Although Stephen, I believe, mentioned this possibility. Again, I didn't know what Mafia meant either. The American Mafia I learned, at the time, to be an organization of crime offering protection practices so they themselves would benefit from racketeering. I was unfamiliar with all or any of these ideas and expressions. I had to even look up the word racketeer. The word itself seemed exotic to me.

The idea of Lee Harvey Oswald acting alone could not be comprehended. The idea of a single-minded person wanting to cause so much anguish and mayhem was not a consciousness we were at all familiar with. Our thoughts at that time would only allow us to believe in a conspiracy theory or a political organized alliance that would answer for such an intended malice act.

Dad had come home on the weekend and he watched the entire news coverage over and over again sitting alone in the one living room chair, his head bowed down with tiredness. The aftermath television coverage tormented us with the question of going to war. Dad said to us, "I don't believe we will be at war with Cuba over this incident." Dad went on to say how, "The Cuban Missile Crisis of October 1962 had been resolved after numerous direct and indirect communications between the Kremlin with Nikita Khrushchev and President J.F. Kennedy with the White House." Dad said in addition, "The deployment of Soviet missiles in Cuba and the US removal of missiles in Turkey, the two sides had begun to reconsider the nuclear arms race. The hotline was introduced and beginnings of early talks on installation of the Test Ban Treaty had already begun earlier in this year. His question remained, would Vice-president L.B. Johnson, now to be president, carry on with these same JFK policies," Dad told us. "He didn't feel after, all those events in place, that JFK's assassination would bring a further reaction for war."

After and during the next week, the younger teenager girl who lived next door who was Richard's age told me her dad was going to begin to build a bomb shelter. "In your backyard?" I asked. That comment was hard to swallow. I certainly planned on watching him build this bomb shelter. The girl's dad was an insurance salesman with an uncommonly larger belly not only that, he liked his vegetable garden and especially his prized tomato plants. Trying to visualize him building an underground shelter to protect them from nuclear bombs was too far a stretch of an idea. I knew this gal often liked to tell tall stories. Maybe though for once, I wanted to believe my dad was right and so I needn't fear a new war. For me, the worst was seeing the late JFK president's children his son John-John and his daughter Carolyn at his funeral on television. How would that have felt not seeing their father again? I didn't connect this to my life. Their family and their dad portrayed, what seemed at the time, a sincere reason to me why you would genuinely feel his loss.

Chapter 28

At this time as well, Stephen came to tell us he had to move with his mom back East, to Toronto or further East to Nova Scotia, her home province.

Stephen was angry at this prospect and complained he didn't have a choice. He asked if he could come back for Christmas. Of course, that would be wonderful for us as well.

Then, in the first week in December, Alan asked if he could move into our basement and pay us $60.00 rent a month. Richard, and I looked at each other. All three of us descended to our basement. It wasn't finished or decorated particularly well. Although we had attempted with our Uncle George's help when Mom and Dad, were still around to make some part into a room to play table tennis. That part of the basement had paneling and the concrete had been painted so it was pretty nice. Alan was so happy we would let him come and stay with us. I offered to wash down the dust off the paneling for him. I had rarely, until this moment, seen his eyes look so happy. He actually showed teeth with his broad smile. He offered me $2.00 a week if I would iron his shirts. Wow, this was getting good.

Richard said to me that night when we were doing the dishes together. It was too bad Alan wanted to quit regular classes at school. Alan's father had been killed in the Second World War, and Richard explained this meant Alan being his son was entitled to a free university degree. Alan had told Richard he hadn't any interest in going to university. To get his mom to see he wanted to become a boilermaker was to move out and get on with doing just that. I believed we inspired Alan to get going and giving him affordable rent also made it easier for him. He had already been approved for an apprenticeship and he was helping us for sure. For one thing, when Uncle George saw for the first time Alan's face through the window in the garage, he quit coming. Alan was the first person besides myself to hear how scary Uncle George sounded, knocking on the garage door and appearing in the window. On Alan's first Friday night he ran right up to my bedroom on the second floor and whispered what was going on. He was, by his expression, terrified. I started to laugh and told him how we had forgotten to tell him about Uncle George's Friday night prank. Before going downstairs with Alan to the basement I shook my head at turning on the light to go downstairs and placed my finger over my mouth gesturing be quiet. Uncle George was still banging hard on the garage door window. Alan now looked at me and put his finger up to his mouth and nodded. He began moving crouched down and kept lower than the garage door window. Then, being so tall, when Alan reached the garage window, he suddenly stood up on his tippy toes looked out the garage window and shouted, "Boo!" Almost immediately our Uncle George stopped pounding at the window. Uncle George had left on his headlights in the driveway, they were just enough light to startle him by the sheer size of Alan. Alan then returned to his crouching position and we returned upstairs. Once we arrived in the kitchen, Alan couldn't stop laughing about how my uncle had actually scared him. Alan then introduced me to boloney and Velveeta cheese sandwiches.

Chapter 29

Now with the new arrangement in place, with Alan along with school going well, the lunchtime drop-in group varied but continued. The student council meetings were tolerable. My shyness in public continued. It was if I couldn't quite believe my peers didn't see through my exterior and see I was actually living by myself with my brother. Nevertheless, we had the scheduled date confirmed for the upcoming 'after school' dance in early December. Volunteers like myself would be on hand to sell tickets at the door and help with both the set up and clean up. Art students were approached to volunteer time to crafting posters for the dance. Their posters were opportunities to use their own creativity. The art students surprised us by using early psychedelic artistic images. I couldn't myself interpret their simple message at first with their very distinct swirling patterns.

This social occasion settled. I looked forward to another invitation. I had been invited to see the folk singer Gordon Lightfoot sing at the Cellar. I had no idea what this would mean for me. But Dennis, whom I had gone on a date with in late May before my mom and dad left had, asked me out for this event. It was being held on a Sunday evening. He said the evening wouldn't run late and I didn't have a curfew, although I imposed midnight on myself anyway.

This particular December evening, the weather was clear. There was not even a raindrop. I was able to wear my new penny loafers, black knee socks, and black turtleneck. I had taken sewing in school this past term. I had purposefully made myself a new plaid wool skirt with black in the plaid. My home economics teacher, who couldn't get my name straight, called me Thelma. My teacher, who stood mainly at the front of the class rather than offering any real assistance, made the following point on my behalf. "Thelma," she called out both sternly and loudly. "This is a beginner's class and it doesn't include learning how to sew in a zipper." But I persevered asking a good sewing student for help so I could give myself a new outfit. I myself wouldn't even have understood the concept of changing to a zipper attachment. My sewing skills were still so rudimentary.

Dennis picked me up at 7 p.m. We arrived to the sound of a local guitarist playing. The lighting gave the Cellar's place a beatnik atmosphere. It was very unconventional. I was mesmerized. Dennis was writing and reading a lot then and I was an attentive listener. He was enthralled by what Albert Schweitzer had accomplished. Albert Schweitzer had been an explorer, of life. After graduating from university, Albert went back to school to receive medical training and became a doctor. He built his own hospital in Lambarene, located in The Republic of Gabon. Dennis had written down some of his many inspiring quotes in his journal. This particular one he had read out to me, "A man is ethical only when life as such is sacred to him, that plants and animals as that of his fellow men, and he devotes himself hopefully to all life that is need of help." After Albert Schweitzer started his hospital, he added an additional wing to accommodate people suffering from leprosy. The disease leprosy wasn't understood at that time and the toll it took on communities was disastrous for those it afflicted. This certainly felt to me like not only an act of kindness for mankind but would have taken great courage as well.

Albert Schweitzer was a hero to Dennis. In 1952, he had won the Nobel Peace Prize for his book, *'Out of my Life and Thought'*. He certainly had earned being a humane doctor. Margaret Mead, the American Anthropologist was a heroine to me. She had gone so far as having to learn foreign languages to establish her knowledge. Through her personal experiences she authenticated how different persons lived in their cultures. She documented the beginnings different cultures took in developing communities. How, although all communities were fundamentally the same, they still differed from ours. The different recognized inherited societies living now in North America had been influenced by industrialized Great Britain and urban European cultures. My dad had bought us her book written for children titled, *'People and Places'*, and it had opened a door for me to be curious about the beginnings of societies and how they survived. Definitely Dennis and I shared a philosophy together to have kindness for the misfortunate and the misunderstood. We had coffee and apple strudel with whip cream. I had never had this before and I was in awe how simple this was and yet unforgettably tasty. By the time Gordon Lightfoot's upcoming folk guitarist, was introduced, the place was packed. Gordon Lightfoot sang his ballad, *'The Canadian Railway Trilogy'*. It had not yet been recorded, nor had his song *'Early Morning Rain'*. I was taken in by this new way of listening to music. I was indeed thankful to not have to share my new living arrangement because of the music. I don't remember if I told Dennis on the way home how my life had changed. I don't think it would have fit with the mood.

Again, Dennis took me home around 10 p.m. He had no idea I had just turned thirteen. He had just put together I wasn't in high school. Neither was Dennis, he had graduated high school a year earlier.

Chapter 30

The after-school dance, coordinated by the student council went well. We, the younger student reps, directed our time arranging cookies and pop. I was really into this social event. The regular couples danced and I was my usual wallflower self. The music was good, the homemade treats were tasty and the cleanup with help wasn't so difficult either. Soon after this, school was about writing essays, tests and results, and then Christmas Eve was upon us.

Christmas Eve, Alan hung around in the early part of the evening before he had to go and visit his mom and sister. Richard wasn't around, no word on Dad coming home or not. By this time, I was reading a lot, so back upstairs I went to read.

I went to sleep earlier than I had thought I would be able to sleep. I became wide awake with a big commotion downstairs. I figured Richard and Alan were partying it up, so I didn't worry so much and managed not to go downstairs before 9 a.m.

I went absently into the living room and I was immediately surprised. On the floor near the entrance was Stephen in his sleeping bag. Across in the dining room I could see someone else sleeping, it was Kate.

Stephen woke up immediately and I was so happy. What a great Christmas gift! He told me he had taken the bus all the way from the center of Toronto, Ontario, Canada. He wasn't with his mom at this time for some reason. She was in Nova Scotia. He was the best gift ever! I was so familiar with not understanding my own mom. Why would I question why he wasn't celebrating Christmas with his mom? Stephen was the person who continued to support Richard and me in our independence whether he was aware of this or not didn't matter. He liked being with us.

Kate objected to the conversational noise. I retreated and went in the bathroom to prepare myself for the day. It was going to be an okay day no matter what happened now.

In the past, Christmas was tolerated. My mom's favorite thing to do was to decorate the Christmas tree. We always had a blue spruce fir tree at least six feet tall. This was the most traditional part of how we celebrated Christmas in our home together. My brother Richard helped with this tradition and so it became important to me as well. Richard and I would decorate the tree. We would take time to lay the strings of tinsel on each branch painstakingly. I enjoyed his company immensely during this activity. It was a happy time together with him and Mom. My mom's second thing was shopping for us kids. We did get some very lovely gifts, new clothes, a doll, or a game. Once in a while a special gift, like when my mom bought me a portable forty-five record player that played by using batteries. She even included some vinyl forty-fives. Popular tunes by Lesley Gore and Ricky Nelson. These gifts from her were appreciated. Again, once when my sister had completed her airline course and moved to Vancouver, she had bought me a light blue skirt, blue vest, matching shirt, and blouse. Or my Auntie June bought me a doll and made all the doll clothes for it. *Wonderful.*

The only thing was by the end of January our mom took them all back and we had none of the things we had previously received. It would be explained to me I was too old for the doll. Or the outfit Kate bought wasn't the right color on me. Or it was too expensive to continue buying batteries for the portable record player.

So, Christmas without gifts was fine by me, no need to worry about what would be taken back. The stupid part was that the gift didn't have to have been from Mom. Anyone's gift given to me from any relative was returned if it had value at the secondhand store or could be refunded.

Later that morning, Barbara called and invited me over for Christmas snacks. I couldn't say no to that, but I first wanted to spend time with Kate, Stephen, and Richard before I went.

At Barbara's, we sat in her formal living room and had tea and home baked cookies with Christmas cake. I realized that this was what most of my peers would be enjoying in their way of celebrating Christmas. It was such a contrast to the past few months. I enjoyed it immensely. I was comforted by their generosity to share a real tradition for them with me. I enjoyed listening to the carols on the radio being sung. I loved observing their happy faces with the telling of what they had received, new underwear and bath salts. The warmth of the house alone was inviting. Then it was time to go, I walked back to my house in my new warm coat. During the short walk home, I was thinking how it would be far reaching in the memory of my mind, if I even tried to imagine any past Christmas at our house having this amount of lightheartedness being shared between siblings and relatives.

The rest of the day and the following were terrific. During these couple of days together we ate well and even had a fire in the fireplace. Dad put in an appearance then, both Kate and Stephen were gone. New Year's was approaching and with happy regards for the New Year from my uncle and aunt on the phone. I was happy enough. Richard and Alan decided to have a New Year's Eve party and I retreated early as not to disturb.

New Year, 1964.

Chapter 31

It seemed odd to me that I was still not in contact with my siblings or my mom, but back at school. Dad told me it had to be this way while he and Mom fought over the child support issue. Dad was all about Dad. Whenever I walked along the beach was when I felt the greatest loss for my siblings. I don't really know why, as we hardly ever went to the beach together. But that was where I truly missed Thomas and Amy. In some ways, it was too horrible to think what their lives might be like in this moment anyway. I liked to think they lived in a nicer place than we did living in this house here. But it was probably doubly sad both their sadness for us and ours for them. I would sometimes wonder, if Mom's forced move was, well intended. Had she wanted to protect Amy and Thomas in a way she hadn't protected Richard or me? Certainly, if Dad wasn't seeing them, they were not being exposed to his abuse. If she had hinted in anyway why she planned her getaway from Dad. I would have gone with her for sure and supported her intention. But the times were not for talking about these subjects. I remember, once I had complained and complained about having a sore vagina. I even went under the scope of both my aunts' examination of my vaginal area. I was seven or eight years of age. They had a discussion in the kitchen together. After I had dressed, they pulled me aside and told me, along with my mother watching my expression with her arms folded, I had to stop drinking orange crush. That was their solution.

The weather was wet, and miserable, my wool coat was hung up to dry each day, in our bathroom with no heat. I had no umbrella. Dad was still resistant to turning on the heat. I complained so much he finally was considering a heating blanket, but when? I am surprised Alan living in the basement doesn't complain more. When I find Alan eating his breakfast with his comforter over his shoulders I complain on his behalf as well.

School is much the same but I am able to skate at the downtown rink now on Friday nights. This is my entire social life. Thanks to my neighbor who gave me these skates and thicker socks I borrowed from Alan out of his laundry basket. This might not seem like a lot, but if you live alone without family, there is very little social life during the week and including the weekend. The empty house and the constant having to do everything by myself is unnatural to how a teen is supposed to socialize. I seemed ant-social, but I just had a hard time knowing what to talk about and how to fit in. I learned to ask questions about everyone else's life and be genuinely interested. Alan coming to live with us allowed my brother to be rarely at home. Alan and Richard would go out on the town with their peers. No explanation just whatever felt good for them to do. Alan being able to drive and having his own truck was a real treat I suspect for my Brother to join him.

After Easter break, the weather improved. Barbara asked me if I would skip school and go and watch the movie *'From Russia with Love'*, a James Bond movie. I was excited to participate in this adventure with Barbara, as I had never even thought of doing something like this.

Barbara liked to skip school a lot, and her parents had helped by including movie tickets in her stocking for Christmas. With the movie cost being free for us, we needed only bus fare.

With my $2.00 allowance from Alan, I had money for the bus and we even went to the five and dime store. I bought a pink lipstick and Barbara later showed me what she stole while I was paying for my lipstick. Stealing didn't seem necessary, and yet Barbara got a thrill or something from it, similar to missing school I suspect. I was thinking when she was telling me about her stealing, how I never wanted to threaten my living situation further. It seemed a treat her being able to do something like pocket an item. I am sure she didn't see it in the same way I did, to attention getting.

Before we gave our tickets for the movie, Barbara had me put on my new lipstick. I was so happy that the movie theater let us in, and we watched the movie with the theater almost entirely empty. Once inside, Barbara explained how we had to look older so that we wouldn't be caught for missing school, since the movie theater could call the school's truant officers. I guessed then I had indeed taken a risk with my situation. The movie was wonderful! Totaling escaping from my life was great. Taking the bus both ways was an added adventure. I actually had the opportunity to see where the public library was and intended to use the money from Alan to come down and get books frequently. By this time Dad had taken the T.V. and given it to a girlfriend of his that lived here in Victoria. I still hadn't put together entirely that this was where our dad was residing when he came to Victoria.

Chapter 32

Today, I am sitting on the toilet looking out the window at the peach blossom. Soon the peaches will come ever so small in the beginning. It is so quiet in the house. I am alone. The sun is brightly shining through the window and the bathroom is clean. I have finished my Saturday chores with my brother and I am sitting here because I have cramps. I am taking my time.

Two strong memories come over me while I am sitting here on the throne. When I cleaned the bathroom weekly for my mother, I used the product Ajax and scrubbed the bath, sink, toilet, and floor. The small mirror over the sink as well. I became quick at it, and by the time I was twelve years of age I had been cleaning the bathroom weekly for over four years methodically. The problem was my mother didn't like it if I finished cleaning the bathroom sooner than she thought it should take to clean. As I became faster at this job, I still had to remain spending time in the bathroom. I had to estimate and wait until the time she thought it should take to clean. I didn't wear a watch so I didn't know how long this cleaning time was to take. I would take a book into read. I would leave the window ajar. If I heard someone coming down the hallway toward the bathroom, I would throw the book out the window and collect it later in the day.

One day, she surprised me and brought in the bathroom with her both the book and yardstick. Right away she started beating on me and telling me I wasn't to be reading on the job. Now crouched over, sitting here cringing, remembering my mom's behavior ridiculously angry because I had taken these steps to filling in the time by reading. The bathroom had been cleaned. She didn't complain about the condition of the cleaning. On top of beating me with the yardstick, she forced me by slapping me on my cheeks to give up my mouth piece. It wasn't enough to hand over the bridgework from my mouth at the time. I had to be continuingly slapped across my face and hit on my legs with the yardstick. If I didn't appear to cry and feel like it was so awful, she would keep the appliance with the teeth for an additional amount of time. So, I acted out my tears cornered up against the bathroom window but really after years of beatings how could I still cry.

The feeling in the pit of my stomach today is about the betrayal of Richard my brother who found the book outside and reported it to my mother. Sitting and remembering this and having my teeth with the metal plate back in my mouth not having to worry about further accusations ever again, allows my monthly cramping to subside.

Since this activity of beating me occurred regularly I had blocked out the most horrible memory when I was ten. My dad came up to my bedroom in the middle of the night, closed the door roughly, surprised me by telling me to lie on my stomach and then lay on me.

I remember the initial pain but then I went very still. The next morning when I had woken to feeling drenched in wet stool and blood. My pajamas were ripped at the crotch. I went downstairs and saw my mother was sleeping with my dad. I asked her gently if she could help me because I was bleeding. Mom's first response was anger because I had woken her then said she would meet me in the bathroom. I remained at the doorway while feeling wetness and watched for any reaction from my dad before I left their bedroom but there was none. I knew he had heard me enter. How could I stand up to Dad when my mom wouldn't even stand up to him?

I tried to explain to my mom that something had happened to me but I saw she was powerless and couldn't help, even if I explained in detail what actually had happened to me. I came to this idea of her helplessness as I watched her peering at herself in the bathroom mirror. She was at the same time explaining to me how I was having my first period. I wasn't sure that I knew exactly what that was but I told her I was bleeding from my backside. She told me that was just how it might feel. She gave me a Kotex pad and one of her elastic holders. She adjusted the straps for me. She told me I would soon see over the next five days. Mom never enquired further and I never bled from my vaginal area. After three days, the bleeding at my rectum stopped. I had been ten years old at the time. I didn't get my first period for another two years. After that, I would often sleep under my bed if I heard any loud sounds downstairs or any loud commotion. The smell of the wax polished floor with dust bunnies would remind me to mop under my bed. Not only did I avoid my dad by sleeping under my bed but also unexpected beatings from my mom. At that time my mom was working shift work. If she came home and found Thomas had peed in his bed, she would blame me and come up and beat me. Now continuing to sit here, I sighed in relief. I felt peace taking in the spring breeze while the window was ajar. My life was quiet. It was a blessing Mom, Richard, and Dad weren't here.

Chapter 33

As the spring of '64 turned warm in May, I became friends with Geoff and Ron, both in my grade eight class in physical education. As a class, we were spending a great deal of time outdoors with sports activities and we were able to socialize more in lineups for broad jumping, high jumping, and relays.

Geoff's home was located near the school and we the girls of our grade eight class were invited to go back after school to Geoff's house to play a game of pool. Geoff had dreams of becoming a marine biologist and living in California. Ron, his friend, was more like me, still pondering the idea of the future and what it could offer. Ron said his brothers were trying to influence his decision of what to pursue. I found I was more of a listener of boys and their dreams. I had trouble starting a conversation with any of my peers on expressing a desire to have an education beyond high school. It's not that they didn't have those dreams I am sure they did. But they wouldn't share openly about them to me anyway. I learned how to behave by boys and my brother's friends. I learned to read and have conversations on politics, cars, and travel. In contrast to our spoken dreams of the future, Geoff's mom would stand at the top of the basement door and yell about chores he was supposed to have done. Folks did everything to get you to do stuff around the house after school. This interpretation of course had changed a great deal at my house. Geoff was very personable and was able to get a varied group of kids to his house on a regular basis after school. It was a lot of fun just hanging out. The girls would talk fashion, favorite singers while watching *American Bandstand* and the guys played pool.

Chapter 34

Ending a school year, I wanted to earn money over the summer holidays. At age thirteen, there was still nothing with the exception of babysitting. The neighborhood kids who used to go berry picking are now old enough to get better summer jobs. I don't feel safe going berry picking by myself. I had learned you needed protection at times by being with older teens or rough behaving kids would take what you had earned. They would claim the pails of picked strawberries you had picked that were left for picking up to be weighed were actually their pickings. I had learned on lunch breaks these particular pushy kids had to help with the daily living requirements for their families' households. They had to meet a daily quota of earnings each day, no excuses.

Barbara and I are walking on the beach boardwalk, a rare treat now with summer's arrival. Already fourteen, Barbara is starting to work in her dad's office this summer doing filing.

Early on during a weekday summer afternoon. I was reading Margaret Mead the anthropologist, one of her books from the public library, *'Coming of Age in Samoa'*. It seemed I could be reading girl's romance books but since Mom and Dad had moved out, I couldn't relate to imagination of that sort any longer. I hadn't any romantic feelings as a young blossoming girl now. I couldn't feel anything in relation to my body and the changes that were occurring. Listening I could hear our phone ringing. I answered to the Hudson's Bay Company's department store was asking if I could be available to come in and be photographed in their sale summer clothing Ad. Are you kidding? "Yes," I answered, I would come. When I was still twelve and living with my mom, I had taken a make-up course at the Hudson Bay department store over Easter break. They had seen my finished photo from the make-up course and thought I might have the right look for their newspaper ad.

I arrived eager to take my part. I didn't have a clue in what to do once I arrived and the photographer fellow didn't seem to have much of an idea of what he needed from me either. I struck some poses and he told me to face him or move in small ways while he took photos. I had to change my garments and periodically I found myself taking gasping breaths during the time spent being photographed.

The company person supervising the ad gave me a check before I left and I now had money to buy some clothing for myself. The company person was kind enough to explain if I took the check to their bank, I could receive the cash. Recently, the money from Kate had been more infrequent. I would take the long bus ride out to the Woodward's department store in Mayfair Plaza. Then ask shyly if there were coupons in my name. When the second time in a row the answer was no, I quit taking the bus. I didn't feel I could expect more from Kate. Walking away the second time from the mall I came to accept the gift was over.

Summer days were taken up by lying on the beach. Then, in the evenings, Barbara and I would walk the boardwalk and watch the older kids mingle. I had used the new money from the modeling job to buy myself a bathing suit and towel. The problem with being so long in my torso was finding a one-piece bathing suit that fit, meant getting a woman's size bathing suit and it included a formed breast cup. As usual, I knew little or nothing about the gravity of looking like I couldn't even possibly fill out the top. Everything I learned about my own sexuality came from my father, brother and whom I dated. Girls were reluctant to share at all with the exception of becoming pregnant. Even though I read Margaret Mead's book *'Coming of Age in Samoa'*, trying to use it as a guide for my development I didn't learn any practical applications that I could apply to my circumstances. In the book, it spoke of girls supporting one another and aunts along with mothers helping through what I was experiencing as the awkwardness of my life with puberty. As I was walking to the beach with a teen boy, already in high school going the same way. He actually spoke to me about the problem of my bathing suit. The exaggeration of the top represented a false me. He had seen me wearing it earlier in the week. After seeing how embarrassed I was, he immediately recognized I hadn't done it intentionally. Although I was stopping at a very different area of the beach, I noticed a change when I went to buy myself a popsicle at the concession. Leon must have passed on my message of how I had come to buying this bathing suit and promptly stares stopped. I had been so naïve I hadn't even noticed the staring until I had this conversation with Leon. That evening at home I cut out the formed cups and it felt good doing what would make me be more real.

In a simple culture such as Samoa, you were treated as accepted in most cases rather than having to go through a competitiveness that our provincial town culture seemed to promote. This idea of competition seemed funny to me because the question I would ask myself, what have I got to compete with? None of my life ever held a thought of anger or hate toward these teens they were my mentors they were what I looked up to fit in and to be normal. Everything Richard and I did was intended to have acceptance for us to be a part of our community. Our life was invisible to all adults around us. I was beginning to see how our life was too strange to imagine.

Chapter 35

One day, I was walking alone by myself on the main street, Beach drive. A fellow came the opposite way riding his bike on the sidewalk. He stopped and introduced himself as Robert. I was surprised by his intrusion. Robert's very short conversation included inviting me to have tea at his house the following day. Although I don't believe Robert meant to come across with a semi-formal invitation. I felt with his British accent, along with how he dressed. Gray flannel pants in summer? It was a strong indicator I would have to dress for the occasion. I had to figure out a way to remind myself to be on time.

The day of the invitation I had chosen what I thought would be appropriate wear. My only sundress with sandals, I had to walk of course. It was hot and so dressing up didn't make me feel overly comfortable in being myself.

Robert's family house on Beach Drive was set back from the street. Walking up the driveway path, the worn exterior was softened by the drooping roses colorfully adorning the front stairway. I was interrupted from this thought with a greeting from David. I had not met David yet and I did not know that Robert had an identical twin. I knew instinctively that I hadn't been invited by this fellow, but was at a loss as to why I knew. David, of course, had been expecting me and so this was the uneven circumstance that I encountered.

David, although he did not introduce himself, did take me to the back and into the kitchen where I was introduced to his mother. He then stated he would go look for his brother. The aging woman had a tanned face. It was a stark contrast to her sons who were so fair skinned and looked like they had never seen the sun during the day. Despite the wrinkled sun weathered skin, she did have the same clear blue eyes. Her very white hair made her appear more in likeness with Robert. I was thinking before Robert appeared how I hadn't been in a kitchen with a mother for a very long time. It had a feel of warmth and security. Robert interrupted my thoughts with his abrupt arrival. He was actually pouting while he told off David. He was very upset with his brother for not making me aware they were identical twins. Robert then introduced me to David. The biggest visible difference in these identical twins was their hairstyle. David's hair coloring is more ash blond to go along with his deeper dark blue eyes.

I recognized their specific southern England dialect, as my older sister's spoke the same.

Without interference from their mother, I was directed upstairs to a bedroom. The room was decorated with an easy sitting arrangement on the floor. A stringed instrument, a mandolin I think was up against a wall along with a record player. I don't remember pictures on the wall but I was certainly surprised given the arrangement of being in Robert's bedroom was okay with his parents. After speaking philosophically over something or rather, Robert offered me a Russian cigarette. I didn't smoke so this came as surprise to me. I declined and Robert, not the least bit offended, told me then it was a Russian brand famous in celebrity movies. We discussed the review of movie titles *'From Russia with Love'* and *'Dr. No'* both with actor Sean Connery. I had not seen the film *'Dr. No'* but had seen *'From Russia with Love'*. We never brought up any discussion regarding the women in these movies. We only discussed the action, cars and gadgets. Along with how the Bond character portrayed how British spies appeared remarkable in different plots.

While we were sitting easily on the floor with cushions, Robert's mother came up with a teapot and cups for tea. I don't remember there being any biscuits. Her intrusion startled me. When had my mother ever thought to serve tea to anyone of us kids at our house? Robert was totally comfortable with his mother serving us tea in his bedroom.

After tea and listening to some Russian classical music, to go with the cigarettes I suppose, I was then led back down stairs and shown out the same side door at the back of the house. During the walk home, I felt uplifted and happy I had gone to visit this unusual person.

Chapter 36

A whole another year, has passed by, it was now the beginning of autumn. Beginning a new school year now in grade nine. I would be fourteen shortly and I seemed to have settled into the routine my new life offered.

I had stomach pains the entire fall to my left side. I thought it was like a stitch but it was somehow worse than that. I ended up missing a great deal of school and had to go to the doctor who decided it was my appendicitis but not severe enough to operate.

By the following spring 1965, I had my appendicitis operated on. Turned out by the time the surgeon did operate, it was worse than they predicated.

This precipitated a longer stay in hospital. During my many absences from school, I accumulated poor marks in math and history. The decision, without my consent, was to hold me back a year. I learned this news once back at school. Mom, Dad or Richard hadn't come to visit me in the hospital after my surgery, even though Mom worked for this particular surgeon. Returning home taking a bath and having to wash off the brown colored antiseptic surrounding my incision. I couldn't rely on any help from family. I hand wrote my own notes to be excused from gym.

Weeks of a quiet recovery routine went by, and I observed when Richard laid out the dishes on the dishtowel cloth, we had many holes in the dishcloth. Our towels and dishcloths were old and ragged, and there wasn't a thought on how I could change these things. Our basic household needs just like everything else were not being met sufficiently.

A good wish had come true. I, now, finally had the long hair I wanted because I never had a haircut. It was Barbara who, at that time, invited me to come to the hairdresser's school and have my haircut and shaped. Barbara, at the time, had the notion to get a perm. Her mom agreed but she had to have it done at a discount. I went along and was embarrassed, as the girl who washed and cut my hair found it was so thick, it took her all morning. Finally, the instructor had to step in to help her. By the time I had this completed, the girl had missed her lunch and even Barbara had read all the magazines in the front part of the salon after her perm. This must have been why my mom kept my hair short. Reading these magazines at the beauty school was interesting to me as well. An article in *Glamour* magazine on Jean Shrimpton, a famous British model, was inspiring to me. I felt she was stepping away from how women were depicted in most American magazines I had seen. She didn't even smile. There was strength in that. Just like Jacqueline Kennedy didn't try to falsify how she was feeling since the passing of her husband, Jean Shrimpton was telling me my unusual height, my boyish young woman look was okay. No need to falsify blooming into a voluptuous figure. No need to wear more make-up. A natural look was okay, I wasn't a hippie, I was being myself.

I was blossoming though, and I couldn't wear a sweater or a blouse without my nipples showing. It was Linda in my art class that pointed this out to me. I needed to go and buy my first bra. luckily Barbara wanted to come and help me. She took me to the underwear part of the Hudson Bay department store and we bought my first bra. These things were not pleasant experiences, but experiences that made me feel unprepared for life and left me feeling unloved and uncared for. Barbara, now fifteen and with an older sister, didn't feel the same awkwardness.

I remember being angry with my mom over these issues. My confidence was initially thwarted somehow by these experiences. This is when I would turn back to reading the *'Coming of Age in Samoa'*. Linda, my classmate in art class, had me over for hot chocolate made with cocoa and condensed canned milk. This simple but satisfying drink had me accept how peaceful life could be by just given a daily pleasure. Of course, her companionship was part of it as well. She had only her mom but that seemed better than myself only having my brother. But then it was still thought of being uncommon when there was only one adult in the household. Although now I knew of at least four similar situations where only one person either a mom or a dad lived with their kids. I would lie in these instances and say my dad was living with us. Nobody asked why I chose him over my mom.

I began writing in a diary, which I bought with monies earned ironing Alan's shirts. It was a five-year diary. It had a key. I really liked the locking away my secrets. The only problem was that I couldn't seem to write anything about my days. My days then seemed repetitive and boring. I begin to record the people who invited me out for either a party or a date. These activities were few and far between still.

Chapter 37

My girlfriend Barbara became pregnant during the fall of that year and she asked me if my older sister could get a hold of some quinine. It was supposed to assist in aborting a pregnancy. I, of course, didn't know the answer but I called anyhow. Kate didn't get me some quinine but confirmed it could be helpful. Barbara's boyfriend did get the quinine and rented us a motel room downtown on Douglas Street. The instructions given to us were by word of mouth to assist with taking the quinine was to have Barbara take hot baths and stay with her until the embryo/potential fetus bled through. To see my friend in her helplessness, while in this hot bath, was overwhelming. I was able to go home before any blood clotting evidence of an embryo came but it was a very long day indeed. Taking the bus home at twilight was frightening. So much to keep locked away inside of oneself. Shadows from persons, streetlights or trees irked me on the way home. I, didn't share this adventure with Richard. It was two whole days later before I knew from Barbara the intended process had work. These moments would bring on waves of my feeling both emotional numbness and helplessness. I was fine in school's routines where I could hide from asking myself in any depth what my life really was. At home was when I would feel these waves of aloneness in both my stillness and emptiness. I gave the name of living such as I was 'living in a vacuum'. My actual day-to-day living outside of school routines didn't connect me with any form of reality I had known.

My many years of domestic training allowed me to follow through with what needs had to be done. My conventional provincial thought process was being pushed to accept and take part in responding to social consequences that have trivial meaning in what is believed to be acceptable normal teen life. These disconnected socially unacceptable moments I took part in leave me questioning why finish and graduate high school. I had forgotten how I had pushed to stay here for that very reason. I had hoped for more fun. More persons live in these fringes than our community on the whole wanted to know about. Since there was so little else, I could do, I continued nevertheless. I used the same intuitive drive used by me to complete daily tasks necessary for living with my brother and Alan. I was not interested in being an actual student.

No one took in the seriousness living our daily life. The idea of picturing any future was artificial to me. It was like a line had been drawn and I didn't know or have a reason to cross it. I hadn't any plans for the future and no one expressed any interest in plans for me. Planning my future would have meant impeding the current flow. What was the future other than failing to survive? These interruptions in my life such as helping with my girlfriend showed me how Richard and I lived and helped others not with judgment but with the same means for understanding we had for our unconventional circumstances. My brother and I were locked in a time warp only moved forward by the requirements asked by our school year.

The summer of '65, I met a lot more kids at the beach in the summer and I began dating out of boredom, loneliness, and curiosity. The curiosity was more about what other people's lives were about and how they differed from mine. I found that dating was, for me, having friendships through boys. Although at the time the term platonic was in, meaning in friendship only. Most of my dates didn't see it that way. Of course, I had my 'three-date rule', along with my diary where I wrote all my names of the boys who asked me out. I had to mark down how many times I went out with them and then be accurate about telling them I only dated for three dates. A lot of times I had someone walk with me to the beach and later to school or I invited the person to come to our lunch drop in or if they drove, I was invited for a ride in their car where we might go for an ice cream. I wrote about walking with a boy. I felt the most comfort in walking with a boy if he didn't try to hold my hand. I would often only walk once with a fellow if he wanted me to hold his hand. A fellow who could tell a good story and laugh at himself was the best. A storyteller made it easier on me as I could not tell much about my life or family. If the boy drove his father's car, I wrote in my diary more about his car than the boy. It made for a luxurious moment for me. Our neighborhood was, if not anything else, wealthy for the latest in cars. It was not unusual for me to be asked out by someone who would drive us in a Lincoln Continental somewhere. Sometimes a Chevrolet Impala, or a Ford Galaxie. The seats were comfortable nothing like my dad's Morris Minor. These cars were the latest in style. Barbara's father drove a navy-blue Buick Skylark convertible with a white leather interior. Barbara's boyfriend drove a British Sunbeam sports car. But when Barbara's sister dated a fellow who drove an Alfa Romeo Spider sports car and we were able to sit on the trunk with our feet dropped over into the back seat and be driven around the entire block, we thought it was both fun and extravagant. I stayed away from going to the movies on dates, but by far my favorite was when I was invited out for dinner. Not having folks around to introduce my dates to wasn't too bad, I would lie about how my folks were out at the time I was being picked up if asked. Lucky for me my three-date rule would kick in and I wouldn't see them after that.

Chapter 38

During the school year, I read, walked and kept to myself. I read a book at school called The Chrysalids by John Wyndham. I was so impacted by one of the main characters Petra. Although the book was science fiction it made me think of fantasizing a way out of my current situation. I started envisioning a rescue plan. I was enthralled by the idea someone or something could actually help me. I think my English teacher Mr. MacDonald understood how well-read I was by now and how repeating grade nine was extremely boring for me. Basically, the book acted as a coping skill for getting through the school year. The previous year, I had been in his top group until I had taken so many ill days. I struggled that whole second grade nine year to make attendance a priority. The author Albert Camus and his book, *'The Plague'* had me introduced to the idea of existentialism. Giving me an idea how to possibly re-interpret my world. I had been told to believe in having family care for you, or relatives meet for celebrations to be noted as in having a birthday, Easter, and Christmas. And yes, I had very real moments of love shared. Unfortunately, now Christian beliefs were simply a veneer washed away from my social life. Just as in the story of *'The Plague'* he wrote about how the disease kept both sides of relatives apart physically and therefore life together became a distant memory and then of course future to minimum planning. I too couldn't connect the pieces to my past life. Earlier pagan beliefs had equal amount of value as Christian beliefs. The idea of having a reunion with loved ones was non-existent. What would we even be able to communicate with our activities so defined to only embrace our survival? My brother and my choice along with our dad had given us an exile life creating a barrier to our siblings and a forced existence. Removing the passion to love and celebrate as a conventional family might. But if truth was told, I didn't miss my past life.

Chapter 39

Finally, end of the school year came and I would be going into high school, grade ten in the fall, 1966. Still only fifteen during the summer months, I had limited resources on how I could spend my summer holidays.

In June, my dad introduced us to another teen, Michael who needed a room to rent while he worked for the tourist attraction Tally-Ho. Tally-Ho consisted of horses with carriages giving tourists excursions around downtown Victoria. Michael's uncle owned the business. Richard was upset, but then dad must have made a deal with the money with Richard, because he came around to the idea pretty quickly.

Kate was upset about it. I wasn't sure why, but there was a lot of talk about me having to go on 'the pill'. They were telling me that the birth control pill was going to help with my periods but I said I was fine with the heating pad (my Dad's substitute for a heated blanket) and Midol. I didn't need any birth control pills. My sister Kate started talking to me about the rhythm method. I found this interesting but didn't have any specific purpose for this knowledge at the moment. I did share this idea with Barbara. She had been using it and it had been unsuccessful for her. Barbara told me her menstrual periods were too irregular. I must say her direct answer to my information shocked me. As girlfriends, we didn't usually talk frankly when it came to sex.

I had recently been able to babysit for my old neighbor, Mrs. Granger and her husband. They apparently settled to the idea I was staying and I was older now so they offered me to come and babysit again. Their two sons were now aged four and seven.

Out of the blue, my mom called and said I could apply to work in her office for a filing job. This seemed awkward. I didn't even recognize her voice. How long since I had spoken to her? It was coming up to three years. I attended an interview at her office, but I didn't speak with my mom. I was re-introduced to the surgeon who had operated on me for my appendix a year plus ago. I still blamed him for contributing to having to miss so much school that I had to repeat the year. I was polite when I re-met him but had little additional respect once observing his treatment of patients and staff. He wore a suit and looked like he was going to pull out a cigarette at any moment. He didn't wear a white coat. To me, he came across as one of those characters types I read about in the novel *'Atlas Shrugged'* by Ayn Rand. He saw himself as one of those few good men, squeaky clean. My mom loved him. My mom was under paid why did she insist on seeing him as the one and only. It made me feel sick to my stomach watching my mom speak with him. He didn't cross my mind as someone who would pull himself up through his integrity. Why should he, it was a time when doctors interpreted how they ran their business. Doctors in my mind wrote their own rules still believing in the idea their work was superior. A woman's support in managing their financial books had less need for appreciation fiscally than what was absolutely necessary. My mom's worth was evaluated by what she learned to save the doctors in the office from any additional tax. I knew my mom was both clever and painstakingly efficient. The wages offered to me although a modest amount would help me, with purchasing school supplies, clothes and shoes for the fall. Being thankful was hard for me at times. Especially since I could see through people's sympathies so easily.

I took the job.

Chapter 40

Stephen had been enticing in his arguments against the Vietnam War. We had several discussions along with the lunch drop-in kids opposing the Vietnam War. During the past school year, I had felt lucky to be in his presence to hear these discussions. Stephen began his arguments by being opposed first to what became known as 'McCarthyism'. Joseph McCarthy had made it clear to the public what he felt constituted anti-American practices. The attitude of McCarthyism led to allegations toward individuals that might threaten American way of life. He felt it might help the masses be fear driven in getting support to arrest unpopular people. These supposedly unpopular publicly named persons with their beliefs could be used to create propaganda to heighten fear in American society. Although those McCarthyism days supposedly ended in the 1950s, Stephen would say that those preaching ideologues from Senator Joseph McCarthy were dangers still to be avoided. Stephen made sense of what 'political fear' meant in society. The United States now had J. Edgar Hoover, head of the FBI (Federal Bureau of Investigation). He was frustrated with the Supreme Court not prosecuting registered voting Communists living in the United States. Edgar Hoover then, went into investigating known communist party individuals by having IRS (Internal Revenue Service) audits of their taxes. He would write letters and install planned strategies to continue his belief these believers thinking differently from what he termed 'The American Dream' needed to be brought to justice. His attitude spread and worked in having Americans believe that they needed to go to war in Vietnam and once and for all, end communism spreading to America soil.

A few intellectual members of the May 1965 Second Movement originated the phrase, "Hell no, we won't go!"

I decided to protest the Vietnam War under the suggestion of Stephen who had already left in late June for Ontario for the summer to work. Although his mother had returned to Victoria, Stephen still felt he had the opportunity for more work in Ontario.

I now had a job and yet. I still had free time on the weekends.

First, I asked Barbara if she had any interest in taking part in a demonstration. "None," Barbara replied. Another friend Janet, who at times would show up for one of our lunch drop-in discussions had similar concerns as I did with the Vietnam War. Janet was non-committal, so I was on my own with this idea.

Michael, our second boarder, was a perfect example of seeing how he saw living at our house. When he could see no adult, lived with us. He demonstrated he couldn't take it in and perhaps, because of that he spent very little time at our house. He would glance at me in the kitchen making something to eat and stare and see no one was around and then leave hurriedly either out or into his room. He never said more than hi to me for a number of days. Unexpectedly, one day, he off handedly offered this observation to me as he was frustrated by how his day had gone with what he called 'hippies'. Michael told me how each day a group of students gathered near Douglas Street at the Victoria Empress Hotel harbor launch. Here is where American tourists docked to see the Empress Hotel or were lined up for a carriage ride on the Tally-Ho enterprise, often visiting Canada for the first time. Michael mentioned tourism was hampered by these demonstrations. Not seeing the value in that comment, I decided to see for myself.

I took the bus downtown, on a Saturday something that was easy for me to do now on my own. I walked to the harbor. The weather was perfect. A slight breeze helped with the summer heat. I soon saw the protestors lining the boulevard. I joined them by staying on the peripheral side of the grassy area outlined with bordering flowers. It was my first experience in protesting anything publicly. Although I was shy, I soon was in the rhythm, using the phrase, "Hell no, we won't go!" The well-familiar phrase was indeed catchy. I was instantly engaged. Seeing the tourists surprised faces also seemed to help me build confidence in my shouting. I was not alone. I was with a group of twenty or more. I may have been standing on the fringe of the protestors but I felt included. This time I didn't feel afraid of jeopardizing my living arrangement.

Almost immediately, once finding my rhythm and feeling my confidence building, I was interrupted. I was being confronted by an actual draft evader and questioned sternly. He approached me directly, asking the question, why I felt I had the right to sing a slogan that would not directly intervene with my life at all. First off, I was hardly able to distinguish in my youth at the time between a beatnik, groupie, and or hippie and never considered I might have to actually engage with a draft-dodger.

He had come out of nowhere with that distinct smell of incense and hashish I smelled on Stephen many a time. His long hair dirty, was invasive to me and I stopped shouting anything. I was sufficiently frightened by his appearance and opposing voice. He then explained with his voice raised for others to hear beside myself how he didn't feel these protests were going to help him. He was an American exile with a landed immigrant status in Canada. Now I was taken aback by these remarks.

For myself, this was one of my first ever worldly experiences where my action was not wanted as I had imagined.

This draft-evader had sufficiently scared me enough for me to remove myself from the group and I sat with him on the grass of the boulevard and heard his story. He was indeed one of the first Americans to immigrate to Canada and flee before receiving his draft notice. Then in the summer of '65, become an actual war resister. His personal conflict with his decision would include being the first generation of immigrants from the U.S. not comfortable in maintaining and embracing their own nation's identity.

At that time, there were only a few hundred Americans in Canada coming up from Seattle, Washington, and crossing the border from Blaine into Canada. These men were unclear of what Canada could offer and they themselves, still angry and feeling distorted to what purpose they could have in Canada as a landed immigrant. Once a landed immigrant, they had to relinquish all ties to their American heritage. Although I too was only a landed immigrant at the time, it was hardly the same for me as I had come to Canada when I was four years old with my mother already a born Canadian. I, in fact, had the opportunity for dual citizenship, having been born in England. I didn't mention it to this young man. After returning home that particular day, I was left confused with what I could do in protesting the Vietnam War. I now had my first experience of using my personal effort in trying to change someone else's idea.

Chapter 41

First days on the job, I found intolerable. I sat near a window on the floor that faced the sun, it was hot, stuffy and I had the boring job of re-doing the doctor's office filing system. There wasn't much I had to pay any additional attention to until I was faced with re-doing the letter 'm' records. The staff made the suggestion I ask for help when I approached the letter 'm'. Every day I would have coffee with the staff as it was in the same room where all the file cabinets were kept. Trying to stay awake was amazingly difficult. The staffs' conversations could not have been further from my life than if you were to ask me how the aliens on the planet made their way through traffic on a Sunday. Luckily, nobody asked more than what school I attended. My mother drank her coffee, listened and said nothing. Not surprising with me at her side. At lunch, I did them a favor and went out to the park right across from their building. Fell asleep and woke up in a panic to make it back to the heated non air-conditioned room to continue until 5 p.m. So began my working life.

During those summer days of '66, I became aware that through my thought process I literally had no identity in respect to my family roots. Even with this job in my mother's office, I had no sense of our relationship or my identity within my original family. I no longer saw myself as what would usually be described as a daughter, a sibling of my brother, an older sister, a relative or a cousin. These terms were in name only. I didn't have a relationship to see or visit with these persons. I had not attended Anglican services since I was a child. All those coined Christian phrases, they had no personal relationship or meaning to me. I had nothing personal to connect me to any community organization. I didn't see any further dependable support for me in our neighborhood. Here at work, I could be anybody's daughter or student needing a summer job. I felt justified with not having my family, political, or religious influence deciding my ideas regarding the Vietnam War. I had established a new society of brotherhood with my brother, the most adult person I could rely on, and our boarders. I still hadn't come to understand completely these persons I actually lived with were, in fact, my new family.

Yet at work, I couldn't speak to any of the persons I shared most of my waking life with it was so not normal how I lived.

Shortly, thereafter with my meeting with the draft dodger, I ran into Robert and I told him about my experience. He was curious about my interest in the war, and again invited me back to his house for tea the following evening.

This time when I joined him, he introduced me to his friend named Trevor. Trevor would be becoming a student at the University of Victoria in the fall. He had demonstrated against the Vietnam War with the students there. I didn't mention I had myself attended a rally earlier in the year at the university. My experience at the rally had been as an observer. I watched students protesting. Although, I had been glad the students were engaged I believed the students were more in conflict with their parent's restrictive beliefs rather than what was actually happening in the War. The draft-dodgers who looked older amongst the students were well-spoken. Their outlined speeches reflected their education. I would learn that they had in many cases established an income here in Victoria through scholarships, grants, or help from their families. In my limited understanding the teens from lower income families or students not supported in their decision were more at risk. The youth at risk may not have been able to afford university and had difficulty supporting their daily living. I felt their anguish as they often looked weathered by their living circumstance. They still felt strongly about the need to protest but were represented by the news as the social stigma face of being anti-war. Again, I observed how fringed lives were not readily accepted in the provincial way of thinking. I understood the well-educated were necessary to Canada's economic growth. I was finding though the fringes in our society's diversity as defined by woman at risk at becoming pregnant, draft dodgers, hippies, beatniks, folk telling musicians, and artists. Trevor went on to tell me how many of these students along with young adults were gathering and living together in communal farms around Victoria. He said they were trying to set up a new way of life to come away from the political upheaval of their homeland in United States. Books popular to encourage this transition Marxist and his little 'red book'. The book *'The Cardinal'*, namely reflected the Pope's hidden secrets. Also, the book named *'The Trial'* by Kafka. Books I was familiar with. These youths living in these communes wanted in Trevor's description freedom from religious, institutional and regimented beliefs. They wanted the freedom to decide what was morally right or wrong with the Vietnam War. Their folks having served in the Second World War assumed their sons needed to defend United States the way they had. The draft-dodgers along with the hippies, commonly bonded as a group were examining the nature of injustice in society and trying to find some kind of solution to it.

During one of these visits at Robert's house in July, Trevor again invited me to spend time at a commune. The next step from these discussions was I willing to spend a weekend at a farming community commune? The commune at the time meant individuals coming together to live an alternative way from their strong Christian, Catholic, Protestant, and Anglican beliefs of our childhoods. If I had thought about it at all I would have been able to state clearly to Trevor I was living a fringe type of existence at my home as we spoke. Only my brother and myself actually monitored our daily lives. Did I want to test what Christian beliefs were still entrenched in my actions?

Chapter 42

Back at work on Monday, I needed to decide if I would take it upon myself to go to the commune for the weekend or not. It was funny in a way, I had only to think it through myself there wasn't anyone to share this idea with. Here amongst the staff at coffee was not a place or time to bring this idea up to anyone sitting in this room.

I couldn't have said anything generally or specific to Mom. Our lives were so strained by our forced paths. Since nothing had been resolved or apologized for, no new opportunity could be presented.

Each person would think I was clearly out of my mind to consider going away with mainly strangers, or even worse, hippies. Deciding factor, Richard had now taken to going to Vancouver on weekends and staying with our uncle and aunt so he could add practice seaplane flying hours for his private license. Looking at another weekend in the empty house, I felt I could agree to Trevor's idea of staying at a commune for the weekend. Having something to plan for made for a quicker work week. When I said goodbye to the staff on the Friday, I was actually smiling. I was being picked up at 6 p.m.

Although, my core for self-preservation was born out of my self-inflicted near drowning incident, I was now going to embark and expand on the need for knowledge for my self-reliance.

On our way to our destination, I couldn't remember if I had told anyone else where I was going or who I would be spending time with. I lived too much in my own thoughts to remember to do these kinds of things. I tried calming myself, as the drive very quickly appeared unrecognizable. Once we left Patricia Bay highway, we were headed somewhere into the farmland of the interior of Vancouver Island which, to be honest, could have been anywhere. I believe it took relatively only an hour, at least two. The heat of the day persisted making it difficult to know exactly how the time was going. I was astonished by how much conversation would take place with stops along the way, yet we were never hurried in our steps. Moving with what seemingly had little purpose but at the same time a certain companionship was present. I hadn't had this kind of interaction around me before. No sense of competitiveness. At each stop, the guys took their time to shake one another's hand when they greeted each other. They cared about what each had to share, whether it was offering an idea for cooking a new different vegetable, they were selling at their fruit stand, what musicians were coming to town, how a mutual friend was in town, or how someone was asking for help with a car repair. These ways of offering emotional, practical generosity were not easily relatable to my life. I initially felt impatient to get to our destination, but why? I didn't know if the place we were headed was better than this present moment. This was my first knowing a peaceful presence surrounded me. In this short journey to our destination, I was awakening to what it felt like being led. Here at this moment, I hadn't any control yet I wasn't feeling anyone pressuring me with force or hostility. No one was even asking why I was even coming along.

When we arrived mid-evening at a fenced in area, the landscape looked completely unfamiliar to me. As we entered the property, we could easily see an old grayish clapboard roof building while driving up the dusty gravel path. The size of the building led me to believe it could have been used at one time as small living quarters for a family. This was where we stopped and parked the American sedan car. We jumped out and the view was immediately very attractive and beautiful at dusk, in its isolated surroundings.

In the near distance, I could see smoldering fires and women on what looked like the main pathway to the creek. Many of the women we passed along this pathway wore their hair braided down their backs of their long summer dresses. I saw crochet shawls draped over shoulders, sun tanned skin from the sun showed through their open weave patterns. I was led down to the creek where a communal laundry area could be seen drying on the overgrown bushes. Here, in these outside surroundings, unprotected by anything I could relate to, I instantly felt even more restricted than my fringed life. I took a deep breath. I had nowhere to turn back to ask anyone, or mention I hadn't any skills I might need for preparing to be here. We were moving away from the creek and walking toward a very large canvas tent. I felt panic. Near the path, a woman by herself was baking clay beads at a small open fire to sell at a nearby fruit stand. A woman who joined us in my walk nearing the fire was offering to give me a description of how this was done and very willing to press this opportunity onto me. As I was left behind with this woman, I began to feel paralyzed by my decision to be here. I raised my eyes to tour the horizon, at the same time catching my breath, trying to calm myself down further. I saw many women engaged in activity to produce different crafts. I became aware of their friendly exterior response with my presence. My curiosity took over my fear for the moment. Then quickly ebbed back to feelings of distress when two of the women who now approached became invested in me giving an opinion of their craft. They were looking for wanting to be rewarded with praise for their efforts. Perhaps, even to have me purchase an item. I began feeling their underlying competitiveness. With this pressure to give an answer I was drawn back to my own feelings of familiar discomfort. Pressure to please so as not to put myself at risk. Their crafts included beading, sewing by hand small fabrics together to make bags or purses, or using a loom to weave fabrics from their yarn. I was feeling genuinely frightened by their means to earn money to keep themselves supported in this unconventional way. Or was it too much an unsatisfying course of action for me to relate to? Underlying their friendliness was a purpose to their end, freedom. It felt fearful to me what their living situation was requiring them to do. I couldn't take in this alternative way to make a living. I couldn't even take in their fabric choices or designs. Who would, in fact, have the means to purchase their art pieces? Maybe their work would be catchy to a wider audience if they had knitted a sweater? This thought I had was from a privileged way of living. I lived without pressure to sell any purchases. This was far too overwhelming for me. How patriarchal and provincial I was in both in my view and response. I was still enjoying in my fringed living arrangement what I believed were customary arrangements for exchange of goods and services. I didn't then have any words in my vocabulary to support them. I hadn't lived with girls who knew how to support each other. I had only my boy views through their periscope lens for their future. I was pulled up by the crest of their wave for me even to exist as I did. My expression on my face was telling. It was then they chose to leave me alone.

Sitting at the fire-pit, I had a flash back to when Dad took me to a deserted area just outside of Duncan where he was working as a social worker at the time. Duncan was located fifty kilometers from Victoria. I was ten years old at the time. Dad during the summer time set up a tent and campfire area in an open otherwise wooded area so he needn't always return to our home in Victoria during the week. Dad had somehow talked me into coming with him. My other choice was facing another day of my mom's continued home chore drudgery. Even though I had never enjoyed any outdoor activity with my dad ever alone, I decided to go with him. As soon as we arrived at his campsite in the early morning, Dad dropped me off and went to his work. I now had to entertain myself until he returned. I felt extremely isolated and frightened. Again, the feelings of having to overcome unknown fear were paralyzing my movements during the day. It felt the same to me as being alone in our home with Dad. I couldn't take in the surroundings in the area or the beauty the meadow offered because my time was thinking about how to survive this ordeal. Now, alone in isolated surroundings, I became aware if my dad wasn't planning on abusing me in some physical way he may go so far as using a teasing hateful approach to teach me something I couldn't fully comprehend. I certainly had never thought of spending time alone with my dad as safe. It took everything to overcome my fear and decide it was in my best interest to make a fire and cook something for us to eat. Making an outdoor fire was indeed foreign to me, but I had learned by watching my brother how to start a fire at home in the fireplace. Deciding to find matches by going through Dad's stuff in his tent was the scariest. Inside the tent was hot from the sun, Dad's belongings were smelly and on top of this the thought of being caught doing this, I didn't believe Dad would believe my good intention. I was never in my opinion heard when I spoke on any subject. When it came to Dad, I needed to complete a task before ever being believable. Once I had those matches in my hand, I began feeling more relaxed. Opening a can of beans, and heating them in a pot. Cutting up bread and cheese, I could manage. Dad's cheese was moldy of course, his favorite, made me laugh. I cut away the moldy parts for my meal and left the cheese as it was for Dad. I worried about our water supply. I counted the water containers and canned goods. Then I watched the sun to estimate the time my dad could possibly return. I had no appetite. When he did return, it was early evening as I had predicted. I felt initially relaxed when he came out from the trees. His presence showed me nothing to fear. He looked tired from his day. His tie had been loosened and his wool sport jacket was over one of his arms. The meal I had prepared was ready and he ate it, with no questions on how I had spent my time. I witnessed him grow very tired after his meal and retire himself into his tent. I made up my bed by the open fire. He took me home the following day. He may have only wanted my company and the meal on this trip, but I could not believe that would be enough. He didn't speak a word to me driving the forty-five minutes ride home, Dad was in his head with his problems. Sitting in the heated car as he drove, silence was the only comfort I felt in his company. I felt the same vulnerability here at the commune. I didn't have the memory of any real pleasant recreational experience to fall back on. Because even when my dad was driving me home, I was still trying to protect myself in my mind from possible events that could have occurred. I was still scared of him. Now I was thinking here at the commune what actions would be necessary from me to survive this weekend?

The following morning, I found the women I encountered on the commune wanted to genuinely offer me the freedom of the outdoors and to enjoy myself. I was hesitant I could barely take in the beauty from these surroundings. I didn't feel safe enough to continue to enjoy it. What was there to do in spending my time here? I still hadn't made peace with what an open countryside had to offer me. My mind was robbed when I was with my dad so long ago as it was being robbed here now. My fear was running my thoughts. I was projecting onto this experience, thinking I was up against a possible further betrayal I may need to escape from. The same thoughts from the past came hurriedly into my mind. I couldn't live in any present moment with my dad. Just like with that overnight camp out. I was witnessing the same behavior in myself with these women. They did not appear to be free in their daily living and therefore, I didn't feel a bit free in my observation of them. No one suggested taking a hike or even a walk. They were fixated with preparing and meeting their daily needs. The true fondness of the surrounding natural beauty was lost on me. I had agreed to going with my dad. Yet, I still had to live through the discomfort of actually doing it. I believe these women were in a similar predicament of what they had initially agreed too and believed was freedom. It became interesting on reflection to me how our peace can only come from our thoughts. If I had while living with my folks enjoyed the outdoors with them perhaps, I could have relaxed more here with these women. My self-doubt was actually interfering with my ability to be peaceful. It was again my challenge. Unfortunately, from my limited perception I was observing perpetual survival. The women at the commune appeared trapped in their minds. It was not necessarily by their circumstance, but from not truly understanding what would have to be necessary in overcoming their daily challenges. Their upbringing hadn't necessarily prepared them for the physical obstacles they would need to endure.

Leaving your folks or religious beliefs is one thing, but starting a new way of living needing additional skills for living off the land was certainly beginnings in pioneering, when men were no longer the hunters. To me, these women looked trapped in their new circumstances. But they weren't, they were free to go as I was. Why was this obvious to me? I suspected my many years of living survival even before these recent years living alone with my brother gave me an understanding for what could lay ahead of their choices. The women I met were perhaps, also new to having to bond with different women's backgrounds. I was prepared to be loyal to my brother, as I knew him well and the understanding, I needed to have his support. He could be trusted under our new limited regime. But having to trust the different women to come together in kinship for the community, now that alone would be difficult to me. Looking back, if I had not had my experience with my family, I may have possibly been too trusting. As the day progressed, I found myself being hopeful these women would recall or remember how they could overcome the obstacles that lay before them. I was not witnessing solutions of substance at the moment. I was limited in my thoughts as I still lived in a man's world. The possibility of accepting women's ideas to have a new way of living was new to me.

Right now, I knew I had a roof, food and clothing I was conscious of my living limitations. There weren't any thoughts I could bring to help them. Perhaps, they were well aware of their limitations. This weekend was giving me the perspective to see a different kind of protection I lived while living with my brother alone. I tried to breathe and see the beauty and accept the similarities we both envisioned for our future, freedom from our stationed past. As the time past, I was reminded of times when I was a gentler, understanding young girl. Here in the wild life, along with the sheep, and chickens were intertwining a landscape raising my feelings of how I had enjoyed playing with my younger siblings.

Chapter 43

Once I had familiarized myself with the general area, I did not see the persons or, Trevor whom I had come with to the commune. I was on my own.

By the second evening, I learned how to gather fresh lettuce leaves from what looked like shrubs and herbs to make a salad. I had seen the communal kitchen and was impressed with the soup that was being made daily. It did smell inviting. It was a grounding force for me. A woman showed me how they saved the vegetable peelings to make the broth for the soup, although, I was reminded of the scarcity of what was available. I did see sheep and had thought we might be having lamb or mutton to eat, but they were planning to find ways to shear them for the wool. I remember first thinking and salivating with the possibility of mutton, and then quickly pulled into my head. *Do not think about your hunger,* I reminded myself. The few chickens could provide eggs for breakfast. The gathering of the eggs was also difficult if the chickens were not happy with the person collecting the eggs. The cleaning of the eggshells took time and these repetitious activities along with the conversations of panhandling, shoplifting, free love, all that was further creating an internal conflict for me on their behalf as well. Many of these women and men were in pursuit of building a community within a community to belong to. I could relate to their desire to make it work.

It reminded me of when I was ten years old and I was interested in sleeping upstairs in a room across from my brother's room. My brother slept upstairs, but he was afraid of the dark. It made my mom angry. I told her I would sleep upstairs. At the time, I was sleeping in my room with my youngest brother alongside my bed sleeping in his crib. He would wake me early in the morning to be attended to. My mother did move my bed up into the bedroom across from my brother but nothing else. I tried to make my room comfortable and inviting but it was impossible. I used old apple boxes to form a shelf, and it irritated my mom. She did not even find me a reading light. No pictures, even my clothes were not allowed upstairs initially. I would read with the overhead light in the room. Although my mom did nothing to encourage my stay, I was allowed to remain in that bedroom because my older brother stopped complaining about being scared of the dark. I did form a bond with my brother over this and a brotherhood had begun, although it was never spoken. I had spent many years since I moved into that room and let go of any expectation for it to become more inviting. The only good thing about the room was how the uncovered windows allowed the bright sunshine in each day. The view I could observe from both my bedroom windows was a comfort as well. Sometimes, I would just watch out the window at the activity on the street and tell myself that my life would change just as I would continue to grow. It wasn't apparent at the time to me, but my brother and I were building trust and the beginnings of any new society according to Margaret Mead the Anthropologist. Margaret Mead's definition is the pairing of individuals as the natural internal humanness before new ways of living in groups are formed.

The limited available infrastructure or absence of familiar forms that might be considered needed at the farm to sustain the commune was familiar to me immediately. What was to become of them when the fresh produce was done for the season and without regular income and warmer shelter even with each and every one wanting to pull together and make this new life reminded me of trying to make my room into something with limited means to do so. Yes, we both had been given fundamentals, but it didn't lend itself to becoming a freedom either of us could readily preserve. A question came to me had organized religion and overbearing lifestyles with their folks been the only force for these women to make them want to live a fringe way of life? Had it been worth it for the men to escape the Vietnam War? Maybe the lives of these women and men living before coming to the commune had been intolerable as mine had been. Thus, the purpose to not return to those forms of life would be reason enough to find sustainable ways to continue this way of life.

Again, I questioned myself did these women and men have a window to look out from to see purpose that would encourage them to willingly carry on while they surrendered their past desires? Would they let go of scheming, as I had with my limits in changing my bedroom?

We both were not able to turn back in our minds. Yes, we could leave our present circumstances, but although I had been frightened to be in the dark, I had decided to stay in my new bedroom. These women and men were staying for their personal reasons as well. Their reasons for the formation of a commune I could not understand by myself entirely at this time.

A common goal to come together as a group was necessary. An individual could be at risk.

Was this what felt like their restlessness? My own restlessness had taken over of course. I now spent my time trying to imagine a successful outcome for myself as well as them. One idea heightening their conflict was the sexual revolution we were experiencing. Both women and men were seeking freedom sexually. But according to Margaret Mead, all new societies begin with pairing of individuals and then move to groups and then perhaps a progression to starting families. She suggested out of this formation, a natural leadership would prevail in a new community.

I could only register the physical limitations of the situation at this time. A further restlessness may well have been that women and men were not wanting to settle to old ways of coming together but to form a new society coming away from the dominance of a patriarchal leadership.

My brother and I were another form of the natural humanness to survive in a new way. We had grown by having new persons come and sharing our accommodation and we had learned to fit into the larger community. My brother and I were into pursuit of growing up equally and moving on from our childhood.

Chapter 44

During my stay at the commune, I realized I didn't feel I had to manipulate getting my needs met on most things like food and shelter, because I knew my dad wanted to keep the house at the time. Also, Richard my brother was the person who made sure we never went hungry. Those two reasons kept me out of the feeling I lived entirely for survival. I may have found the food choices were limited, that was too bad. It was great knowing there was food and shelter to be relied on.

It would have been impossible if Richard and I hadn't bonded. We wouldn't have been able to make it work. Although we were not great at communicating beyond our needs, Richard and I had an underlined trust together.

Misunderstanding the true nature of humanness may have reflected back from the commune as restlessness. The unsatisfied individuals took to napping, drug taking, and using their own music for ritual dancing. I couldn't see how these alternative choices would work for me. Their sadness at these times was noticeable to me.

The commune and I both faced frugality in our daily lives. Would it lead to freedom of thought and ways to live with less dependency?

Yes, my life could indeed have been described as living in a hippie's commune. One similarity between myself, and the commune was, I wasn't looking for intervention with leadership or another's person's authority. I was presently sailing with direction from my intrinsic compass.

The revolution these individuals were expressing appeared to also be coming from within themselves, and their beliefs. This common thread I had witnessed with both my brother and Dad not being able to completely relax with how we were getting by. It may have been I was not aware how oppressed I was myself. I wasn't being forced to take on religious or political beliefs. But then, I couldn't know my own limited Anglican beliefs and how coming away from a nuclear patriarchal family could open a different barrier to moving forward either. I didn't recognize that having little materially translated to less societal conventionalism for myself at the present. My definition of freedom at the moment included the ability to not stake a claim of how things were to be in the future. Sitting on the grass chewing on a blade of sweet grass, I was having to think what the future held for me. It was difficult seeing how taking your own limited ideas, past thoughts, and trying to use them in limited practical ways, wouldn't necessarily improve my future. For me to have a true understanding of their new chosen life, I would have to not be attached to the hippie's commune outcome as seen through my own provincial upbringing. I was, at that particular time, more attached and fearful of their outcome than my own. I was not fully aware the commune represented a reflection of my own fears for my future. I felt I was simply developing my own terms for making decisions. My small steps taken out into the world were a work in progress. I was trying to learn abilities to own myself.

I slept, ate, walked, and talked my way through the weekend along with giving a helping hand. I grew anxious, impatient and concerned that I would not get to leave. But I did get asked on Sunday afternoon by one of Trevor's friends if I wanted a ride back to town. I was so glad to be able to go. Even though it was dark when I came home to an empty house, I still felt relieved. I felt lucky I had our stove to prepare a steakette patty along with corn on the cob. And I had my pick of fruit from our backyard fruit trees. I picked plums, a peach high up on a branch unreached by my brother and an apple. I maybe living a fringed life, but I was not in any way capable of following in the commune's footsteps.

Chapter 45

Walking into work on Monday, immediately each person in the office noticed I had a sunburned face. At our morning coffee, a staff member asked how I had spent my weekend. I was tired from my experience and felt I hadn't thought about a pat answer to a direct question regarding my weekend. Of course, my mom was curious as well. My mom actually turned her head to see my response to this woman's question. My brain went to a memory of when we had a babysitter as a kid, Mrs. Brook. I remembered her son had a farm and kept horses as well just off Metchosin Road, approximately fourteen miles outside of Victoria. I had stopped at a fruit stand on that road, so I said I had spent a day nearby their farm. I knew my mom well enough to see her relief with my answer. Someone then interrupted to say how the fruit and vegetables were so good right now. Why did I feel I had to lie and protect my mom's reputation in front of her colleagues? No one even cared whom I had spent time with. Such a very periscope view of how a teenager might spend their time.

During these six weeks, Dad had decided now I had a job, he didn't need to supplement our supplies needed from the confectionary store anymore. I went crazy when I went to the store that week and found out Dad had, without telling us, stopped our account. I didn't need Richard to fend for me. I waited until Dad came home on the following weekend. When I saw him coming away from his car before reaching the front steps, I ran outside and started tearing a strip off him about his women, his sailing, his boat, and holidays. I spoke loudly that he had to keep up this account as he still didn't provide any heat for us and he had further income from two boarders. All that yelling in a quiet street reversed that situation. Yes, I could indeed use confronting tactics too! More than likely though, Richard finding out this himself, about Dad shutting down our account at the corner store had his hand in the reversal as well.

Now on the Saturday, I had found out an old movie theater right on Oak Bay Avenue had been turned into a dance disco before renovations would begin in the fall. It was expensive to get in at the time, half a dollar. You could buy a glass of pop, and of course, all the most popular kids from Oak Bay came. As the summer progressed, I found I could go with anyone, as I would usually recognize someone I knew there and I could dance by myself or with someone, nobody cared. This was truly a great outlet for me during these hot summer weekend evenings. It was just a few blocks from my house and the neighborhood police station. I felt safe walking back home by myself and my thoughts were filled with having just had a lighthearted time for myself. My mom suggesting, I could date had been perhaps, her way of offering me a similar way to have fun. But I had experienced the pressure to be someone's date was often oppressive for me at times. It was interesting how my fringed friends wouldn't come to these disco evenings. Neither would my peers from school. These pre-college types were somehow off limits. I could walk from one side of a group of kids to another with no feelings of attachment.

Because of my circumstance, I didn't feel I had beliefs that would make me balk at defending a particular code of behavior for a single-teenage girl. I was naive for sure!

Everything I was coming to believe was determined by what I learned through my actions. My determination for directing my own moral conduct was through what I personally felt and experienced. I had been blinded by my circumstances thwarted in being able to apply myself to a usual teen life. I had to rely on my own force of strength, my feelings were rarely thought of by myself, or others. After my commune experience, I had to seek more social ways of expressing myself.

It was during the warmer part of this particular summer, I was asked by Robert to act out the strategies of Machiavelli's book, *'The Prince'*. *'The Prince'*, written in the early 1500s, was a book that was dedicated to Lorenzo de Medici, Italian Statesman and Ruler of the Florentine Republic during the Renaissance. The author, Niccolo Machiavelli, who was Italian, had been exiled from his country. To regain favor, he had written a small book on power how to gain it, how to wield it, and how to keep it. I felt his tactics were non-conforming. In truth, I had no idea when not following the rules of war, how that would play out. Robert had many toy soldiers and thought we could head to the beach plan out our strategy and attacks and see how practicable these ideas would be. I couldn't remember in any detail how the book, *'The Prince'*, went in any specific manipulative strategy, so I was planning imagination when I played my part. The whole thing seemed surreal to me but I turned up anyway the following Sunday. Although both brothers had agreed to come, it was soon evident it was only Robert and myself. I arrived at Willows Beach dressed more comfortably for myself than for Robert. I found Robert already setting up the many armies of soldiers. I looked around to see if people were watching but no one was paying attention. He chose a somewhat secluded part of the beach that was still near the main walkway. Most people used the main walkway only to head toward Cattle Point.

I quickly became engaged with the setting up the pretense game as I found the level of detailed uniformed soldiers distracting to my ideas, as they were nothing to what I had known and played with my brothers. Robert's very in detail dressed military soldiers could be placed in formations under sergeants, majors or generals. The game of laying out the forces correctly was serious to Robert. I had little experience playing with soldiers in any depth with my brothers I felt forced to play out what I remembered in war stories. It was great having the engagement of imagination so fully immersed with not just myself but with Robert's perception and his in-depth knowledge of that period. Machiavelli's reasons for traditional wars failing and the reasons why wars were successful amounted to divide the masses so that you may conquer them; separate them further so you can rule them. Not always accepted by traditionalists at war. I came away from my imagination for a moment to recognize how I had been brought up to be a believer in wars.

Then I noticed how the very bright sun was in contrast to Robert's very pale skin. I couldn't believe he had ever been in the sun this long. Up to now I was feeling purposeful in my movements. But when Robert moved his men toward a traditional conventional action to take charge of the front lines, I reminded him that perhaps because Machiavelli loved his country so much he would have invited his countrymen from the fields to help in his defense and from these outside forces would have probably over thrown Robert's intended traditional move. This was in my imagination there weren't any men to play out this part in the game. Still watching Robert moving his men into retreat I went on blindly speaking out and pointing out that in the book *'The Prince'*, Machiavelli's aim in conducting a war hadn't been intended to have him necessarily receive glory. I wasn't feeling any emotion behind my words at the time. I hadn't thought of winning for myself. I was unprepared for Robert's abrupt ending of our game. He could have easily argued with me that we didn't have imaginary figures to tip the game at war. I would have respected that argument. I had not noticed his bike or his satchel for carrying the soldiers, but very quickly he had them all gathered up and was intending to be on his way. I felt somewhat uncomfortable being left there, but then this was often my life at this time where I played my part as best as I could and being forthright often left me to being alone.

I had to remind myself, to be less critical on myself with how the game ended. Standing up not sure what could be said between us. Then not looking up at me Robert asked, "Would I be available to come to the house again for a luncheon David was hosting for a few friends in a fortnight?" This description with his choice with language always had the habit of surprising me. It was right out of the time warp of the children's British author, Enid Blyton books. I walked back to the house somewhat tired from both the mental activity and hot sun.

I began to answer for myself the question, why did the Vietnam War have such an effect on me? I realized that I related to the death of so many young men through the personal experience of not seeing my own siblings. I, too, was experiencing a death of young persons. I would not get to see my two siblings grow up, and that was a further loss for me to endure.

On my way home, I ran into my friend Janet, she has similar concerns as I do with the ongoing Vietnam War. She looked unwell. I asked how her summer was going. She had been unsuccessful in finding a job. Her mom was trying to kick her out of her house. This seemed desperate. I suggested she could come and stay with me if things got too rough at home. She blurted out she might be pregnant. "So, what if you are, you can still come." I said.

She said, "It's complicated because of who the father is."

"Okay," I replied.

Janet said, while tears ran down her face, "My mom is going to have me receive shock treatment rather than face who the father may be." My mind couldn't accept what she was telling me. I tried to intercept and re-state how she could come and stay with me. My mind jumped to Janet really didn't understand how I didn't have any adult authority living at my home. How I could have her come and stay with us? Even though she would come for lunch she didn't really take in that no father was coming home to help me with dinner. It was increasingly easier going public because no one actually found our situation believable.

I told her if she came and stayed, we could see if there was any other way this could be handled. She was so anxious she couldn't take in what I might have been able to offer her. I couldn't get through to her she was too frightened for her life. I wasn't able to understand how her father couldn't help. It was walking home alone in my thoughts when it began to sink

148

in what part her father had in this problem. I started to cry. I couldn't help her.

Before actually going to the commune, I had no conscious pursuit in finding further security, safety and comfort. It wasn't available, and somehow, I wasn't able to state my needs or see beyond my daily requirements. Now, I felt like screaming this was so wrong. Religious ideas, philosophy, existentialism none of it consciously knowingly influenced how I could relate to my being able to change circumstances at this particular time. I was living having to passively gather information.

Chapter 46

Another two weeks went by and then off again to David's luncheon with his friends, Robert barely made an appearance. David's friends were all into smoking Russian cigarettes, but the air also smelled like how my brother's friend Stephen always smelled as well. Pot the shortened name given to the Mexican/Spanish leaf, Potiguaya or marijuana leaves had been smoked maybe prior to my arrival but was pungent nevertheless. Incense was burning in the corner of what I believed to be Robert's room.

The conversations while in Robert's room were reflecting the music playing, folk songs by Joan Baez. Joan Baez's own songs were her own personal reflection on how to fight against the Vietnam War. I mentioned that I had attended a demonstration and then was quickly asked what I thought of the hippie movement. I didn't have any political opinion, nor did I want to hide behind a political idea to make a stand against a particular war. After visiting the commune, I was more aware of the aftermath of how persons felt strongly enough to establish themselves to live free from societal beliefs that would insist they had no other choice but to go to war. No one ever asked about how I lived, and really, I could perhaps be thought of living like a hippie, freely doing as I pleased. Yet, no one thought I was making a statement of any kind. I am living with the consequence of standing up after a violent act that had been directed to me personally. Of course, I had to remind myself, they didn't know how I lived.

I mimicked the words I had overheard Stephen say, how it was important to stand up against the establishment, if necessary. But really, I had no knowledgeable practical answer to connect my circumstances to the labeled hippie, or draft dodger's decisions. If I now stated how I lived, people's facial expression would be too much to take on. Although labeling hippies because they joined together like a family, were supposedly easily recognizable because of their hair or the way they dressed. No one asked how coming to their individual decision to help themselves and their peers escape an injustice. How crossing the border didn't actually reflect how they were still patriotic to their own country. When they had to give up their American citizenship to remain in Canada, it didn't change their values. I lived everyday trying to make sense of my world. I am sure these individuals did the same.

I then felt overwhelmed by the room's pungent odor and took it upon myself to leave and go home.

Chapter 47

The following week after I had finished working in my mom's office, I received the most unexpected follow up phone call from my mom. She called to inform me that the shoe store named Mondays had a summer sale.

I thanked her politely and hung up. I did take the time to check out Mondays' August shoe sale. First, though, I took the time to purchase material to sew a new skirt for the fall. Even though I didn't know for sure if I would be granted my option choice of sewing before I was actually back at school. I needed to believe I would be allowed to take the class, as this was the only way I could have a new outfit to wear to school. The only pair of shoes I could buy reasonably at Mondays' store shoe sale would take 40% of my entire wages, I had earned over the past six weeks while filing. While doing the math, I took in this was Mom's idea of helping. It was so in contrast to the way I was actually living my life. My mom still wanted me to dress the same as when she had bought my clothes. I was surprised at how I initially wanted to be able to accommodate her suggestion. It surprised me she still had so much say over how I lived my life. It was like, I must have forgotten how she had behaved three years ago, given this suggestion from her to purchase the shoes. Since then, I have been clouded by the generosity of other mothers. But, if I bought these shoes for her approval, then every other item I bought would have to be bargain basement. I realized then, my mom never would have approved of me sewing my own clothes. Here lay another roadblock to us sharing a mother and daughter bond. Finally, haunted by my past with Mom, I forced myself and bought the shoes anyway. I had, in some way, forgiven her by purchasing those shoes. Only then could

I put nagging thoughts of her behind me. I now felt less guilt in why I needed to sew a skirt rather than purchase one.

Chapter 48

I was happy to get a call from Dennis Bolton, he asked me to come horseback riding with him. When I replied, "Dennis, I haven't been on a horse before."

He said, "Beth, I will get a gentle horse for you to ride. The best thing to do is to get to the stables early in the morning."

"Okay," I said. Dennis picked me up just before 7:30 a.m. We went to the stables close to Cordova Bay. We were helped with the horses and saddling, and off we went. At first sitting that high on a horse feeling out of balance, wobbly awkward, I was thankful having a gentle horse to ride. The staff's reassurance helped. The trail led down to the beach and it was pretty, and though it was narrow, the horse was so used to going in this direction, it felt safe to me. Arriving on the beach with the tide still out was instantly scenic. The sun glistening on the water's horizon was breathtaking. Actually, riding on the less pebbly part of the beach made the ride smooth. After what seemed a short while, Dennis said we should give the horses a break. I was just getting into the ride, so I was not so sure I wanted to stop. I got off with Dennis's help and we tied them to a tree nearby. Dennis had surprised me by bringing a sleeping bag and said we could rest in the sleeping bag and watch the sun fully coming up on the horizon. I was not comfortable with his idea. I felt he was pushing on me to do something I had no intention of doing. I really liked him. He had made every date memorable. But he kept his distance in between and I knew he dated a number of other girls. I was going to have to say something. Lying there beside him, I was thinking it through what to say. I didn't feel comfortable with the idea of having sex with him or anyone. I could not fully understand at the time why I didn't have sexual urges. My strongest feeling for Dennis, I would have to say, could be described as a genuine fondness in my heart for him. I feel I hadn't matured to have any real-life relationship, or even have the emotional maturity to toss away my virginity in a morning interrupted by horse riding. What I needed was for us to become the best of friends. With not another thought, we were interrupted by a group of horseback riders. David quickly sat up and greeted them. I was out of the bag and up standing by my horse. The moment of awkwardness was over. We probably rode for another half hour and then called it a morning. After returning the horses, the uncomfortable feeling between us grew in the car ride home. Now my official third date concluded over a couple of years still had to be noted. Looking back, I wonder why Dennis had kept his distance and his feelings he may have had for me were never spoken. We never really found a conversation between us that spoke to our attraction for one another. I couldn't believe in love, it had to be either a crush or infatuation.

It was now more difficult for me to commit to continuing to date. I was always going to have to make this further commitment to myself, to defend my three-date rule idea. I would need the rule no matter how I felt toward a boy. My deserved dignity and my self-respect were only words, but they had to be meaningful for me to remain true to something purposeful. Although, the knowledge reminded me of how lonely this commitment made me. Barbara becoming pregnant again, along with two other lunchtime friends that year helped me to be firm in my resolution with my date rule. I felt disappointed with the memory of Dennis's awkward behavior, although it remained my decision to not see him again. What indeed could I do? I had only myself to rely on. The three-date rule helped me not to become attached to a future I did not want. More patience was needed from me for an opening in how to trust how I thought about any future that could really be meaningful to me. Patience was the key to allowing answers to come at the pace I could process. In fact,

I had moved to accomplishing this by setting down boundaries.

Broken hearted again, I found the remainder of the summer with cloudy days alone in the empty house along with cooler temperatures unbearable in trying to find comfort in myself. The monotony of the food we ate. The endless time at the beach, as my only alternative to no family, no community. The disconnection between my acceptance and what was required daily. Reading difficult to comprehend literature was my only intellectual challenge to my life.

Little did I know I was in fact habitual in living out the basic Christian belief or value to cooperate with those around you, along with the idea to make sure you are responsible in what you take on to do. This common belief to always be responsible would influence me into single mindedness that was not always justified, and was a potential influence for how I would make further decisions. At the moment, my daily life was too specific with attendance at school and my life with my brother, our boarders. I needed to know how this communal influence could lead me to freedom of thought in myself and have the confidence to act on that freedom.

Chapter 49

It was the fall of going into grade ten when I first met Jack. He was younger than myself but still in grade ten. When I first noticed him, he had been leaning against a railing outside on the school's property. As Jack moved away from the railing, he approached me, and introduced himself as Jack. When he started to speak to me, it was quick and to the point of how he had come to observe me. He said, "I have watched you since school started. I love how your hair bounces when you move." Jack definitely saw a different me than how I saw myself.

He then walked me out to the curb where he introduced me to his cousin Alan, whom they nick named Al. Al was older and picked Jack up from school in one of the family-owned cars. We continued to talk to each other while they waited for a friend, also in grade ten, who lived with them named Bryce. When Jack introduced Bryce, I was struck by his distinct paleness and lethargic posture. Al driving allowed us to go back to Jack's house where we could socialize together. They were all about drinking cups of tea and discussing different books they were reading together at the time. Al was non-committal with his opinion. He was a bit of a recluse. Jack made up for that in spades. Al was somehow staying with Jack fulltime and he was fun to be with. Both of them smoked cigarettes. They were truly inseparable. Bryce spoke often using the reference of a half-full or half-empty glass. His opinion spoke often to the half-empty glass. His voice wasn't what I would have described as sad. It lingered more as being somber, irrepressible. Jack did share after one of these moments, Bryce had been diagnosed with Leukemia.

Before long, Jack had me reading the biography of Van Gogh, 'The Trial' by Kafka, and Machiavelli's 'The Prince'.

In my second reading of *'The Prince'*, I would come back to my continued empty house at night and turn on the only light in my room, the overhead light. I read facing the bottom of my bed. I read with dissatisfaction, the content making no sense to my daily life as a young-teenage girl. Jack and my brother had goals and were in school to help them direct them on their paths. Richard wanted to become a pilot, and Jack was planning to be a lawyer. Most of what I read was directed in what young men could do with their lives. I remember recently walking down the street turning the corner to see a gal and her boyfriend meeting in the early morning. Clasping their hands together they walked up the hill to high school, while holding hands and dreaming about their future together, perhaps, I remember thinking that would never be my life. Getting married and having children was the furthest thought from my mind. But what other alternatives were available still didn't cross my mind.

The few times that really were fun were when Jack had me climb or walk long periods of time during the late autumn evenings. Or Jack teaching me the basic skills of sailing. I never once understood or comprehended what I was actually doing, when a new skill needed practice to be learned. I would become paralyzed, frozen, the fear of failing was so great. I could never give myself the time to think it through what needed to be done through understanding first and practiced second. I was, so narrower in thinking and then applying from my daily life. My personal history had relied too heavily on copying others around me. This was indeed difficult to assess, as I had no reference other than I had difficulty doing tasks that were newly instructed. I had difficulty in learning how to sew, using a sewing machine. But now it was showing up again in learning how to sail. I would freeze, and my hands and mind would not help each other. Why did I feel I needed to be some sort of expert to fit in?

Jack later on introduced me to his friends, Brent and Karin. My best ever evening plans were when Jack would come over with Brent and pick me up in Brent's brother's car. We would go to Mount Tommy, climb up the side of the mountain, light a candle and they would offer wine to drink and we would talk and play cards.

On the way home from these adventures, we would often run out of gas and have to leave the car and make it home on foot. Jack would have to stay over at Brent's house. Even knowing the gas probably wouldn't be enough when they picked me up the opportunity for us all to gather, to discuss politics and let off steam through conversation, cigarettes, and drinking wine was the best. My loneliness subsided when I had extended moments like these. They were a rarity that made them just that much more memorable.

Finally, high school seemed to be an okay place to be. I liked my classes and liked all the new faces. It was okay to go home and do homework. I now had the beginnings of surrounding myself with high achievers who had goals beyond high school. I stilled walked to school with Barbara. I missed her terribly. Having had two aborted pregnancies, she wasn't the same girl I knew in grade eight. Her free spirit was being taken over by her parents taking steps to move her to secretarial school. It was hard for me to see her be persuaded by her fear domineering parents. They had her convinced it was in her best interest, given her marks. I couldn't comprehend how their fear of shame brought onto their family was directing their decisions. I saw this behavior with the girl closer in age to me next door as well. She lived in her parent's home. But they had abandoned her just the same as mine had by putting all their efforts in the oldest, more conforming daughter. I could see she was deeply hurt by their withdrawing emotional support in her life. Luckily, my own transition with my new peers and interests were helping me to develop a need for further schooling. I wasn't feeling so very dependent on my friendship with Barbara.

Chapter 50

Dad had, in the past year, officially moved to New Westminster on the mainland. He even moved his boat up the Fraser River and had it moored so he could sleep on it and make his meals. My sister described my father's new social work services position as better suited to him. Since he had been taking meals from her on a regular basis, she saw him more often than I did. Since the separation of my parents, I lived with no parental influence and Dad wasn't someone I would have recommended to anyone if you were looking for help. In his furthering absence, Dad become more interested in providing a variety of food. My dad, never the cook, started throwing unwashed barley, along with unpeeled, unwashed root vegetables, beef broth, some kind of meat, suet, into a large pressurized pot. While cooking, it smelled like burnt food or worse. He had not yet mastered the technique for tasty pressurized cooking. He said that the burnt stench wasn't really anything to be concerned about. Root vegetables were the best for maintaining your health. Dad continued to come over from New Westminster, on occasion. Now he built in the time to pressure cook a meal and leave it for us to eat. He would leave the pot on the stove and go away for three to four weeks at a time. Richard insisted we leave it for him and when he came back, neither Richard nor I had a bite of his food. The stench, when he lifted the lid, was a driving reminder to leave it alone. Dad would have strong words, but he would not allow us to learn to cook anything or use the raw food to make something else. It was his decision, so it ultimately failed. When Dad was around, for a couple of days, still complaining, Richard would put the pot out on the outside deck. Once Dad saw even the seagulls wouldn't eat it. Dad stopped his idea.

Richard, now in his final year of high school was beginning to see his future in becoming a pilot and was much happier overall. Richard was partying it up a lot now at home. It seemed strange to me keeping company with teens who didn't appear to have any goals for the future, but the loneliness must have taken a toll on him as well. For me, I neither had the money or interest in being inhibited by alcohol. Watching how his friends were unable to function after their parties only made alcohol easier for me to avoid.

In the spring of 1967, as soon as we could enjoy the weather, Jack called me up and asked if I would like to journey up Tommy Mountain. Brent, Karin, Al, myself, and Jack would all be going. Al's new girlfriend, San, couldn't come. San went by the name Sandra at school. San's family came from Hong Kong. Her folks were notably strict with her every whereabouts. We saw her only after school. I hadn't seen the crowd since Christmas. We hiked up to the middle of the mountain as there was a plateau with moss and softened rocks to sit on. We had of course with us, a candle, cheap wine, cigarettes, and lots to discuss.

'Atlas Shrug' by Ann Rand was up for discussion and although I had read most of it by this time, I still had no idea why this book challenged Jack and Brent so much. Both were in conflict with the book for different reasons. Jack, as his own person, wanted to have more of a social conscience about people. While Brent's older brother seemed to entirely influence Brent on how things needed to be in the world of engineers and business. It was Jack's dad, an engineer, steering Jack with the opinion that life depended on just the few good minds in business. The negotiations of government contracts needed to anchor business and influence the spending in government. Since most of Jack's dad's business was contracted with the Liberal Party government. Jack's dad worried when Lester B. Pearson, leader of the Liberal Party and Prime Minister of Canada, became surrounded by influencing minority governments pushing for social change. The heavily relied upon better incomes for engineers should not be jeopardized. In Jack's dad's opinion, we were indeed in a midst of a crisis. If any change by the business community gave any consideration to any of Lester B. Pearson's social legislation ideas. During this time, we watched as our Prime Minister Lester Pearson did pursue social legislation for medical care and provisions for old age pensions. If adopted business would be challenged to do better for their employees either by these programs or by assisting government to help with the cost of higher education. But how did this potential view of a crisis differ from supposedly the same good minds cut from the same cloth, influencing the leadership of the Vietnam War, or leading the news media scare fear of the bomb? All of this conversation, failed in any depth of exploration of thought as none of it really gave potential for more individuals to diversify and succeed in their own way. Perhaps once you stood-up openly for your idea you would find both your ability, integrity, strengthened with your knowledge, and move to pursue with confidence. Certainly, Ayn Rand acted as an individual. I liked how Prime Minister Lester B. Pearson kept Canada out of the Vietnam War.

If you had a strong mind did you in fact use it to consider others entirely or just for yourself? No middle ground when reading Ayn Rand. Christianity and or democracy, you were not to influence without your own moral conscious. Moral conscious, alone still left a lot of persons on the fringe of needing help from my experience. Ayn Rand's thinking seemed justified, given Jack's father's thinking in how he conducted himself in business. But now we were having to observe even in business, or university how traumatized persons were when they were displaced like American draft-evaders. Injustice in American politics with the civil rights movement hardly made it into our middle class conscious. I know how I lived in a bubble and so Jack's father's bubble was equally acceptable. I knew little on how to live differently myself. Although Jack and Brent were, in fact, against the Vietnam War, their strong influencing fathers didn't let them express any views publicly. They respected their fathers as staunch hard-working engineers. Their need to have a good rich life was front and foremost for their future. Charities were the normal way to help those who couldn't help themselves. My own father working as a government employee that didn't even seem relevant to their social connections or social conscious. Jack and Brent were actually being groomed to continue to believe that they could be the strong mind to will the way of the future. I wasn't going to argue. Stephen my brother's political friend probably had the same opinion of himself to challenge the government in its way of thinking coming from an individual's need to be valued. In honesty there was room for different opinions. Much change in thinking in business was necessary. I took away from Ayn Rand's *'Atlas Shrug'* both men and women were needed in keeping the infrastructure or status quo by attending university or college and becoming leaders through their convictions for any new progress to evolve. Women still had little more than a footnote in changing their lives. Women had to rely on the good will of men to shape their lives. Until women and children were not seen as dependents a better life for women in our patriarchal social structure could only be realized by more evidence of subcultures springing up. We were a living generation headed for social change for all people. I decided I could listen to these boys' opinions lightly as they listened to mine.

Chapter 51

Once spring came, Jack as Junior Commodore for the Oak Bay Yacht club, would sail race with his peers. He happily competed with different yacht clubs around surrounding areas.

Jack's parents bought a thirty-foot sailing vessel that spring. He was constantly brooding to be given the opportunity to take out the Cal 30, without accompaniment. To me, this seemed foolish but after I saw how capable he was with his friend Brent at his side, it was a treat to be invited out given the opportunity to help sail this magnificent boat and enjoy a very different kind of freedom. Over time, Jack had me come on Regatta's as a spare. I wasn't good under any pressure but I enjoyed the opportunity to practice just the same.

On the last week in June 1967, exams were just over for me a week away before the long weekend for the National Day of Canada on July 1. In the beginning, it had originally been called 'Dominion Day'. The statutory holiday celebrating the anniversary of the enactment of the British North American Act of 1867, later named the Canada Act. The Canada Act was established to give Canada its own kingdom in its own right.

My dad was coming over from Vancouver more on the weekends. He dropped off food, mainly for what he called our lunch program. Then he was off to sail, but for this particular holiday, Dad, for some reason, came on Thursday evening. He had meetings he said in Victoria, before his plan to go sailing for four days, starting early Friday morning. He asked me if I could babysit for a crewmember, he said who needed to practice for the race coming up the following holiday weekend. It would pay $10.00 a day. That would be $40.00. I needed the monies for sure. I asked how many children, one child only. I would have to stay for three nights. Dad asked if I could pack up and be ready to be dropped off early Friday morning.

Richard had just recently left to work fulltime in construction for the summer in Vancouver. My uncle had helped Richard get on a construction site job in Vancouver. Alan, our boarder and friend that lived in our basement, had gone to bed early and he would leave even earlier than I would with my dad.

I packed up my things in the evening, and knew Dad had an alarm. He would call me to get up when I needed to be ready. Dad slept in Richard's bed across the hall.

Up early and off after a quick dress and toast for breakfast, we jumped in his car. We drove past city center, the home he said was located off the Patricia Bay Highway. I recognized the area we were headed for as Royal Oak, but I wasn't entirely familiar with any of the surrounding neighborhoods.

Chapter 52

We arrived in front of the home, an apartment, just after 8 a.m. The mother came to the door. She was young and didn't appear to have much enthusiasm for sailing, but was cordial to me. She had $10.00 on the kitchen table and she said the baby was sleeping. I turned and looked at Dad, "Baby?"
Dad replied, "Don't worry, the child is four months old."

I noted the woman had a telephone. I wasn't introduced so I hadn't learned her name or the child's name. The child I named 'baby' by me.

The woman told me she hadn't had time to get food for the baby. She told me I would have to take the baby to the corner store and purchase with the money, milk to make a formula for the baby. Are you kidding me? Somehow, I was to carry the baby purchase the food, and bring it all back with me. Oh, and by the way, there wasn't any food for me either.

I was stunned. Dad quickly told me I would be fine and they left. The baby woke up and I was at the beginning of my four days. I went and picked up the baby. The baby was slight in her weight. Mom had always had large babies from birth, so I think this is why I noted this so quickly. I changed the baby, put on clothes and noted to myself that there were few choices. I went looking for the laundry room. Having found the laundry all piled up by the dryer, I went back and put the baby back down in the crib to find a long sleeve something for the baby to wear. As I rummaged through the pile of clothes, a large cat jumped out of the bin onto the pile of sheets. The cat was the same color as the white sheets. I was terrified and ran back to the living room. I had never had a cat for a pet.

I now knew I also had a cat to look after. I found something for the baby to wear. I had one bottle of milk left. I heated the milk up in a pot on the stove. I fed the baby and then looked for cat food. No cat food either. This $10.00 was going to go fast. I packed up the baby and looked for a bag to carry things back from the store, but couldn't find anything. The baby squirmed and I soon realized I was out of my depth. I tried carrying the baby with one hand and arm but it wasn't safe. I had roads to cross as well. This wasn't a corner store at the end of the block situation.

Chapter 53

The only person I could call that could drive out to help me was Jack. Al could drive. He had a driver's license. Alan, who lived with me, was at work. I could not find a clock to find out the time, but I would wait for a while and then call Jack and ask for his help. I waited until mid-morning. I had found what I call a travel clock. A travel clock was square in shape and had a hard cover to protect the clock face and mechanisms on the back of the face of the clock. My stewardess sister had shown me hers. I was fascinated by how different this clock appeared. My sister's cover was tangerine-colored. This one was brown, with a gold-metal trim. The clock made me take in more details in the living room's appearance. I called Jack and woke him up but luckily his mom hadn't answered. It was thought to be inappropriate for a girl to call a boy under any circumstances. I told Jack I had accepted this babysitting job, not sure where it was exactly but near an area called Royal Oak, leading off Patricia Highway. I needed to have his help to get him to buy food and deliver it to me. I told him I had money. He said he would ask Al to help, but if Al wouldn't come, he would drive anyway to help me. This would mean taking his mom's car without a license and driving out of town to me. I told him I didn't want him to risk that, but he said he would get back to me. Luckily, the home number was written on the phone. I told him the number and then hung up. I looked in the fridge and cupboards to see what kind of list I should be putting together. I would buy for myself noodles, because peanut butter and jam were too heavy and expensive. Then I remembered that I could put tuna in with the noodles. I played with the baby, mainly holding and rocking and singing to her. I didn't worry about the mess I was making, as once the baby slept again, I would be able to clean up then if I wasn't too exhausted.

Al agreed to help and they set up a time to come and find me around 3 p.m. I had, in the meantime, gone out to see what the actual address was. I put together a list with milk for the baby being the top priority and tinned cat food the lowest priority.

When Jack and Al turned up, I was so very relieved. They first took both the list and money and bought the food.

When they came back, they had a tour of the place and then Al went and sat in the car with the driver's door open in the parking lot and smoked a cigarette. Jack watched me change the baby and then asked me, "Beth, what is that mark on the baby's arm?" We found two markings. Each marking was on the outer upper arm of the baby. They were rough, red, and swollen.

Jack said, "It seems to me the baby has cigarette burns." The markings were the size of a cigarette.

I said, "Who would do that?" Taking in the living room again, I remembered the living room was full of ashtray butts and I became angry.

Jack said he couldn't stay long, but I didn't mind. Now I had food I could make the formula milk for the baby and food for both the cat and myself. I could manage. Jack would himself be sailing both Saturday and Sunday. He said he would call again. He leaned over and took a pen and wrote the phone number from the mother's phone on the inside of his cigarette package. Typical, that would, of course, be with him until he had finished the package. When I made this comment, Jack answered smiling, "Don't worry, I will transfer the number if I smoke this whole pack before you leave here." That for sure was going to happen.

I didn't know what the baby's schedule had been. I lay the baby on a blanket on the kitchen floor while I made up bottles of milk. I hadn't found any pablum or baby jar food, so I felt the baby was still only taking milk. I was starving, and I had already made sure I could find a can opener, so I opened the first tin of three cans of tuna to eat myself. I ate half a can right there in the kitchen. The baby seemed to be hungry again and it had been mid-morning since I fed the baby, so I fed the baby again.

I suspected the baby would eat later in the evening before sleeping through the night, hopefully. The baby hardly made any noise either happily or not. Cigarette burns? Or was this baby just too hungry?

Chapter 54

I decided to prepare for a six-hour schedule. It was now 5:30 p.m., the baby was dozing off. I put the baby to bed. Then, I put out food for the cat and made myself up a large quantity of noodles and tuna to eat. As there wasn't any butter, its taste amounted to dried tuna with clump wet noodles. I added a small amount of milk. Next, I folded up the laundry and slept on the couch with a blanket. I wanted to know where the cat slept but the cat kept pretty hidden so I rested knowing at least the cat had something to eat.

I woke up and turned on the lamp on the side table. I noticed the clock also on the side of the table in the living room confirmed just before midnight. I strained my ears to listen for the baby. I looked in to see the baby was stirring so I warmed up some milk and prepared myself for the feeding. The baby hardly cried out. I went and picked her up and changed her and then had the milk ready to go. She took the milk and fell back to sleep. I returned to the couch and did the same.

I awoke early with the light coming through the living room windows. I started heating up the milk again. No sound yet from the baby. I gazed in and had a look. The baby was awake but did not stir but stared vacantly at the ceiling. I greeted the baby and picked her up. I hugged her and then changed her again and went for the milk in the kitchen. The baby didn't even try to smile, or make noise. She took the milk and fell back to sleep.

I put the baby down and went back to the living room. Day two. This would be a long day if the weather didn't improve. I found the place was too restrictive to spend any length of time in. I was now beginning to feel restless. I took the time to wash myself and brush my teeth.

The cat was purring now, obviously having found the food. I remained alert and anxious. I did not like how this baby acted. It just didn't seem normal. I decided to bathe the baby when she woke up again. The baby was now more alert with the schedule of being fed every six hours, she appeared less lethargic. I took the baby out and walked the baby in the fresh air by carrying her by myself. I noted there were no toys so I picked dandelions and showed them to her and talked about the sky and the clouds and sang nursery rhymes.

Then, before I could believe it, the time to feed her again had arrived. Both of us had an afternoon nap and I helped myself to more tuna and noodles. In the afternoon, I lay down on the couch. I was pretty angry with both my dad and this woman. None of this seemed right. If the baby woke up or made any noise at all, I was in her room getting her up. Her eyes began taking on a more alert look. Again, I fed her and played with her by carrying her around. I even showed her the cat that was now beginning to warm up to me. I then had more tuna and noodles to eat. When changing the baby, I was reminded to apply cream to her upper arms. After feeding her and getting her ready for bed, I found myself happy for a moment with seeing her peaceful face.

Later that night, Jack phoned, "How had day-two gone?"

I replied. "It was much better, thank you for asking." He had begun drinking, so our conversation was short.

He said, "The sailboat racing had been amazing!"

On day-three, I began by doing the laundry, and emptying the ashtrays and making the place tidy. While preparing the baby for the day, I noticed the cream meant for a baby's rash was helping with the sores on her upper arms. The weather improved, so I took the baby outside.

Babysitting both day and night, I really found the time just was about the baby and getting everything organized. There wasn't a T. V.

If there had been real food, I could have baked something but I had no baking supplies and nothing else to eat but what

I had purchased, so I was limited on how I could spend my time. What did this woman eat? I began to think this person wouldn't have had the money to sail. This woman could have been one of my dad's social welfare clients. Damn it, he was probably sleeping with this woman. Man, I had been set up.

Chapter 55

Day-four, Monday, Jack called. He offered to come and pick me up. I said, "Not on my life." I went on to tell Jack, I want to tear a strip off my dad for leaving me here with such limited means and how vulnerable this baby was under these circumstances.

When Dad came with the woman, the baby was napping, it was late afternoon. I gave them both a serious look, while I summarize what I had spent the money on. I had about $2.00 in change from her $10.00. I told the woman how I fed the baby every six hours, bathed her each day. Took her out in the sunshine and played with her.

I then remarked on the ashtray butts and the butt like scars on her upper arms and told her she was not to do that to her baby anymore. The woman looked me straight in the eyes for only a second or two then lowered her head and answered in a quiet voice, she wouldn't. Yes, this seemed right to stand up for someone who was powerless in the situation. Dad had tried to interrupt me. I raised my voice to him and turned and faced him directly. "Dry up!" My dad's favorite expression he used with me. The woman then gave me $30.00 and I said goodbye.

When I got in the car with Dad, I yelled all the way home about how I doubted that woman could sail and she would not have money or time to sail with such a young infant. I wouldn't ever do anything like this again for him. And that he still owed me ten more dollars. Dad came up to my room later in the evening before leaving to go back to the mainland and sheepishly gave me the $10.00 dollars he still owed me. It infuriated me seeing my dad when he retreated, his back turned away from me hunched over and having to accept for myself, how weak in mind my dad was in the choices he made. Had my mother finally seen through her character flaw and truly admitted to herself my father was a predator. Maybe she had, in her way, tried to get us all away from him. Having to process this possibility was indeed painful. Because of Jack's help, I really bonded with him over this experience. Although, my hardened character of keeping heartbreaks to myself remained.

I also had a first step in feeling the value in offering a valid opinion. I had stood up not only to my dad but also the mother of the baby. Yes, this felt right to use my voice for the helpless and what was morally right for a child. But it separated me at the same time from my peers. Having to stand up for someone else was not what was considered common practice with my peers. Besides, promises are often made in the moment. Would this woman really do a better job of raising her baby?

Chapter 56

Later that summer, Stephen came for a visit and shared the new Beatles album with us. It was becoming more popular to have a theme with the collection of songs on an album. The artwork on the cover was interesting as well. All the Beatles were dressed so differently than they had been in the past. The name of their album was *'Sgt. Pepper's Lonely Hearts, Club Band'*.

The song, *'Lucy in the Sky with Diamonds'*, had Stephen enthralled with the openness of a song seemingly relating to a drug named LSD. Although denied publicly by the songwriters, much speculation went into this possibility. Stephen had helped me understand years before when Richard made the rule no drugs would be allowed in our house. Richard referring to drugs hadn't meant aspirin. He must have already known about Stephen's fascination with marijuana or hashish. Stephen had once set me up to take hashish. He had gone to the trouble of baking brownies and he had told me to help myself. The brownies were on the kitchen counter. I was excited. I hadn't eaten any baked goods for a very long time. I took two brownies and wolfed them down. Shortly thereafter, I saw all kinds of images and was surrounded by imaginary illusions. I made myself sit on the floor in the hallway facing the front door. I knew instinctively I was a danger to myself. I shut all the doors around myself, the second hallway door, my parent's bedroom door, and the living room door. I sat there, staring at the front door while watching men wearing United States military cavalry uniforms from the early nineteenth century approaching me on horses. There were cavalrymen riding on horses coming through my front door and trampling on me. I smelled the horses and could hear their snorts. I remember crying and nobody being there to help. I was trying to protect myself from a very vivid illusion. It went on for what seemed a very long time, but at one point I went to sleep on the carpeted entrance floor. I woke up exhausted. Later, I confronted Stephen. I asked, "Why did you offer those brownies to me?"

Stephen replied, "It was the only way to get you to try hashish."

I replied angrily, "Why did I need to try hashish?" Stephen said it would help me loosen up my thinking. "Yes," I said, "now I won't be open to trusting your ideas further." I suspect that wasn't the answer he was hoping for. These events coincided with him sharing his Beatles album. We still had a living room size stereo. It had been a gift for Mom for listening to her collection of Tchaikovsky. Perfect now for listening to this new collection of Beatles music.

Stephen wanted everyone to hear that album. Since we hadn't any other music as Mom had taken all her classical albums, we were a willing audience. The stereo had sat unused as Richard was the only one who might have used it. He enjoyed instrumental music. Stephen insisted we sit on the carpeted living room floor so he could observe our response to his album. Richard didn't argue with him, but didn't seem that interested. He got up and went to the kitchen to make a snack.

I had gone to a filming of a Beatles concert when my parents lived here with us. The film I saw had them appearing the same as when we had watched them entertain for 'The Ed Sullivan Show' on Sunday evenings. Now, they had changed themselves and it wasn't that appealing to me. A few weeks after, we had been playing the new album when Dad was around one weekend. He took it as a need to be appearing concerned for my wellbeing hearing those songs. He soon had me rounded up and took one of the dining room chairs and made me sit in it in the kitchen while he paced around me in the chair and lectured me on taking drugs. Dad shouted at me about how it would be a problem getting a passport if I was caught with any possession of drugs. He told me, "Beth, it will get worse if you tried selling drugs." I sat there thinking. This was to me, again our dad, all about Dad. Dad continued to yell, "Don't you know with the police just down the block, we could be raided anytime?"

I endured until I finally saw a break in his yelling. "Dad, my concerns are more personal than drugs for me, the most important thing would be if you would turn on the heat. If you would give us a food budget where we could eat something different from hot dogs, and steakettes."

Dad stopped yelling, but still paced, he was now bent over in his posture thinking. Dad was probably worried that he was leaving me now to reside with two boarders. Richard now was moving to Vancouver and I would be left going to school here but with only two boarders in the house with me. I was only sixteen, a possible problem for him being a social worker.

For the rest of the summer, I babysat for the neighbors behind us a great deal as the mother, Mrs. Granger, had gone back to work. It was familiar work, as I had done so much of the same activities with my own siblings. It left my evenings free and I enjoyed the reading time or the time with friends.

Chapter 57

The summer pressed on as predictable as a summer can be in Victoria when my dad turned up drunk one evening. I found him in the living room, sitting in the comfortable chair. He appeared to be dozing. I said, "Hello, Dad." He woke up. He then asked as he went and got a glass of water from the kitchen if he could talk to me. I stood at the doorway and watched him drink the water down. He was looking untidy with his shirttail out, his belt undone, his shoes off a hole in the toe of one of his socks. He then went into the bathroom. He came back into the kitchen and I answered him, "Sure, Dad." My dad appearance confirmed he had drunk too much. He began telling me how he was planning to bring his mother over from England to stay here at the house. "Really? How old is Granny, Dad?" I asked.

He paused and said, "I think eighty something."

"Okay," I commented. Then I asked Dad, "Would she want to come?"

"Oh yes," he replied. *Interesting,* I thought to myself. He then went on to say that Alan would love her cooking. This was typical of my generation, where the results were always how men would enjoy a particular situation. Dad went on to say this is how he could keep the house going. This was Dad's plan for when Richard would live permanently in Vancouver. Dad informed me he had already applied for Granny to come, so it was just a matter of time.

Dad, as usual, in this hung-over drunken state went into a tangent conversation and told me how he was acquiring a budgie and would I be willing to look after it. It would be coming from a social service client that had recently died. "Maybe," I said.

Then, Dad gave a sigh. I guess I wasn't giving any enthusiasm to his plan. He went on to say how he never thought how Richard and I would have created an existential existence here in the house. Here again was Dad with his vague thoughts, his language, seriously an existential existence? What did that even mean? I asked him what does existentialism mean. He was upset I interrupted him. He had a tone and said, "Look up Paul Sartre's work," his tone spoke volumes. He clearly thought he had done everything for us in his mind by providing limited provisions with his need to keep his house. He now said he would have to provide heat but Granny would buy groceries. He admitted to me then how he had been resentful of having to be responsible for us. He had intended for us to fail. Dad, in my mind, appeared happiest with himself if we were either suffering or we were helping others through our lean existence. This, somehow, made it possible for him to support us. With little in furnishings, or warmth in the house over these past years, this had built worth for him. Then he said looking down at the floor, how extraordinary under these circumstances we came to run this lunchtime drop-in program he called it. Feeding all these young persons and then taking in boarders. He had felt he had to continue to support us. To be honest this was a lot to take in. He wasn't apologizing. He was stating he had deliberately made it difficult for many years watching us as an experiment. We had proven existentialism could be lived. My blood must have run cold. I began to shiver. As he spoke, it was sinking in how he viewed us having survived a cruel and revengeful purpose for his intellectual means. He spoke how he had the means to destroy us from staying but had decided it was worth the investment as an experiment and, of course, the house. With the two boarders, he had only to come up with the mortgage amount. My dad was now appearing to me as someone who now had behaved equally as selfish as my mom. He then went up to bed in Richard's bedroom. I decided I wouldn't tell Richard. He may have responded poorly, for different reasons. I myself felt paralyzed, having heard his reasons, but eventually went to bed. Again, no one would have believed how Dad had chosen to draw out our exile existence for a full four years. It was just as difficult to relate to as how Mom had acted.

Chapter 58

I accepted an invitation by Jack for the weekend to attend the Maple Bay sailing regatta, now four summers after my mom left. It was going to be a very different August Labor Day weekend for me. I had spent many a time with Jack sailing, over the past couple of years. I longed for the chance to have a real sailing race moment. But, as I was a spare, it wasn't going to happen if the team really wanted to win. I didn't have the confidence in myself as an assured sailing team member yet.

Karin didn't respect me for tagging along on this Regatta trip, but she did at least tolerate me. It turned out, by telling her mother that another team member was a girl she had been permitted to come. Sailboat racing in a Regatta was, at the time, more for boys than girls. Karin would be going to college in the fall. She was one year older than myself. Karin's folks would be paying her tuition. She went to the private school I had first gone to when my mom and dad moved back to Canada. But once my brother could read and we moved to Oak Bay, my parents quickly changed us over to a public school. My life was too foreign to have common ground with Karin, with the exception of sailing. Also, her boyfriend, Brent, was Jack's best friend.

On this trip, Karin and I were sharing a beer at the end of the Sunday day's race in the Cub's cabin. The medals would soon be awarded and this was a moment where the boys were in preparation for the awards ceremony. Karin told me what a drag it had been getting her parents to approve her coming on this overnight Regatta. Her parents didn't let her do anything and this was one hell of achievement. She held up her bottled beer and toasted, "Cheers." Mainly for herself but I joined in.

She then went on to ask, "Did you have difficulty in persuading your folks to let you come?"

I replied, "No."

She replied cynically, "How fortunate for you."

Then with what I noted to myself, as her usual stuck-up self, asked suspiciously, "Did you lie about where you were going this weekend?" That question really made me break out in an unexpected laugh, even for myself. First, her suspicious stuck-up self, with her tone asking, and secondly that was not even in the realm of my life's arena. What adult cared how I spent my time? "Why, per se, is this so funny?" replied Karin.

I had known Karin now for almost two years but we never ever really talked. I answered as casual as I could muster, stating in a soft voice, "I don't live with my folks."

This remark only increased her look of stubbornness toward me. This again, wasn't helpful information for her. As if grasping for an idea, on how to explain my circumstances, she asked, "Oh, do you live with your grandparents?"

Again, I laughed, too surprised at that possibility. "No," I replied. But seeing her impatience, I added, "I live with my older brother."

"Oh," she said, leaning back in her seat, "is he married?"

"No," I replied, adding the sentence, "he just graduated high school in June."

She looked appalled, shaking her head. Now, I felt I needed to give an explanation worthy of her expression. This was making me cringe. Now, what would make any sense to her? I began by saying calmly my brother and I took in two boarders. Saying these words out loud didn't help her to understand any more than hearing myself say them. She then went back to her tone reflecting a confirmed suspiciousness of me. She interrupted me by asking directly, "Why on earth do you not live with your mom and dad?"

I took a deep breath and looked at her directly and said, "Four years ago, on this very start to this holiday weekend day, my mother tried to kill me with a knife. My mom moved out the following day with my siblings, and my dad moved to Vancouver. I remained in the house with my older brother."

Karin, barely taking in what I was telling her, began scoffing with a quip facial expression asked, "How old are you?"

I replied, "I am sixteen."

We both finished our beers without making eye contact. Then, Karin rose, took the moment to flip her black shoulder length hair back, and we both headed up onto the deck. I then remembered I hadn't even told Barbara about my mom's actions since the episode with the knife.

I came to the realization as I remained on deck looking out to sea that I had not only survived. I had grown up using circumstantial experiences. Fortitude had helped me to let go of limiting beliefs, including needing adult supervision. In place of adult supervision, I had used self-imposed limits and my heart as an intrinsic moral guide. More importantly, I had just found my way out of my head with this truth being spoken to Karin. Interesting to me by learning a new skillset to being able to sail, I had embraced my dad's love for sailing. I realized then through our trials, I had come to forgive him as well.

Epilogue

It was New Year's Eve, before becoming 1968, and for the first time I celebrated in a party of my peers. It was fun. Richard had asked me earlier in the day if I would take on flying with him as a passenger in a Cessna 150 on New Year's Day. I said I would. I then had asked Richard if Jack could come along as well. Jack had expressed an interest to have a ride in a small aircraft. Richard said he would be happy and appreciative, as he needed to log his flying hours with different passengers.

The following morning, I was a little apprehensive. I thought it might be the time of year. New Year's Day and winter weather, perhaps. But the weather showered us with a blue cloudless day sun shining brightly. How could I be anxious?

We drove out to the small airplane holding area and left Jack in the office to wait for our return. The plan was, I would go up with Richard first and then Jack would be asked to join him on the second voyage.

Everything with Richard went well. He set himself up, checking his instruments slowly, and going down to the part of the airway where we would join with the main airstrip to take off.

Very soon after taking off, we were up into the brilliance of the sun shining looking at the most beautiful parts of the farming community. We had elevated our aircraft and leveled off. Everything was going well. Richard pointed out landmarks; Gordon Head, the sea outline, our beloved Cattle Point. He was circling over the sea outskirts, within minutes rounding the plane around when he felt the engine stall. I still somehow did not feel much of a difference. He became very serious, looking at his instruments and having to tell me we would have to perhaps be forced to land as he was beginning to lose altitude. He called into the airport, but rapidly became aware he was too far from the airport to actually get there and land. We headed out over the ocean, but Richard quickly said what we needed to find was probably a farm extensive enough to land the plane. As we began to see and approach farmland, is when the engine actually quit altogether. We were just floating we seem to have those similar thoughts where your whole life flashes before your eyes. Only being seventeen, I felt that was a quick minute. Then, Richard caught my eye and said with the deepest regret felt, "I am so sorry, Beth." We were at the time crossing over and away from the highway and with the few fir trees we encountered, we could see they were taller than we were. Then, on the right of me through the passenger window I was seeing a fellow watching us fly. He was sitting on his deck looking out from his yard, at the same time, he was smoking his pipe. It felt I was looking straight into his eyes and caught his startled expression. I then caught him with my peripheral vision getting out of his chair. Next, looking forward, Richard was voicing his concern at how close and in our sight an oversized green house was looming before us. Then with a tremendous thud, we had hit the frosted ground. The plane tip forward before it came to a complete stop in slow motion. We were grasping the thoughts we hadn't run into a fence for livestock or the green house. Oh my, we were so happy. Still, we were feeling scared, we could hear police sirens. We couldn't imagine what they would ask of us first. The first question asked by the police officer as Richard descended from the plane, had he been drinking. Jack drove over to where we were after getting instructions from the airport. Richard stayed with the plane until another pilot could come and assist him to getting it back to the airport. We weren't able to get Jack up in the air that day.

The very next day, Richard went out again. But although the explanation of the previous day's incident was icing on the wings, I was not game to go. I stood my ground and went up later in the year.

The year would bring my grandmother moving out to live with us from England in the spring. Another sailing regatta, this time in Seattle.,

Later in the same year, I would hear through my grandmother on my mother's side that my grade nine English teacher, Mr. Macdonald, comments having learned I was living alone with my brother from my aunt June, working as the school secretary. He couldn't believe I had dressed so well, including keeping my shoes so polished and my hair so groomed.

I would also go on to learn how my dad would tell me how my strength in mind scared him.

All these events and comments would prepare me for my next adventure.

Bibliography of References

Alan Haig-Brown, Hell No We Won't Go, Vietnam draft Resisters in Canada, 1996 Published in Canada Raincoast Books.

Albert Camus, The plague, 1947, Published in English 1948 UK Hamish Hamilton.

Franz Kafka, The Trial, 1925 Published in English after being translated by Willa and Edwin Muir. In 1937 London, UK, by Martin Secker.

Henry Morton Robinson, The Cardinal complete and unabridged, 1950 USA, Published by Pocket Books, INC. NY Rockefeller Center.

Ian Tyson, The Long Trail, My life in the West, 2010 Canada, Published by Random House Canada.

J. Krishnamurti, You are the World, 1972 USA (NY), Published by Perennial/Harper & Row.

J. Krishnamurti, The Fulfillment Years, 1983 First Published in Great Britain by John Murray Ltd.

John Hagen, The Northern Passage, American Vietnam War Resisters in Canada, 2001 USA, Harvard University Press.

John Wyndham, The Chrysalids, 1955, Published in UK by Penguin.

Margaret Mead, Coming of Age in Samoa, 1928 Researched for The American Museum of Natural History as research, Published 1928 USA William Morrow and Co.

Margaret Mead, People and Places, 1959 USA, Published by The world Publishing Company.

President Kennedy, USA Presidential Library and Museum, November 22nd, 1963.

Quote on front page by Henry Wadsworth Longfellow, American, Fireside Poet New England, United States.

Roger Neville Williams, The New Exiles, American War Resisters in Canada, 1971 USA, Published by the Liveright Publishing Corporation.

The prince and selected discourses: Machiavelli a new translation/edited by Daniel Denne Published by Bantam Books New York/Toronto/ London.

Timothy Findley, The Wars, 1977 Canada Published by Clarke, Irwin.